Pride of Lions

Pride of Lions

Brian Bertram

Charles Scribner's Sons
New York

First published 1978
© Brian Bertram 1978

Library of Congress Cataloging in Publication Data

Bertram, Brian, 1944-
  Pride of lions.

  Bibliography: p.
  Includes index.
  1. Lions.   2. Mammals–Tanzania–Serengeti
Plain.   I. Title.
QL737.C23B47   599'.74428   78-50843
ISBN 0-684-15782-9

1 3 5 7 9 11 13 15 17 19   20 18 16 14 12 10 8 6 4 2

Printed in Great Britain.

Contents

Colour plates

Foreword

This book arose from lots of questions. As I drove people around with me in my landrover, looking for and then looking at lions, I would be bombarded with stimulating questions, and, it seemed, expected to know definite answers to them all. 'Why do lions have manes?' I was often asked. 'And why don't they have spots like leopards? What do lions eat? How do you know which lion is which? How long do lions live? Why do they mate so often? How do you put a radio-collar onto a lion?' And so on. Everyone seemed to want to know more about my subjects.

A striking thing about all these questions was that they might be asked by anyone, from the most eminent visiting zoologist down (in height) to my four-year-old nephew; they all seemed to want to know much the same things. This book is my attempt to answer them all at the same time, as well as to stimulate many more questions. It is intended solely for the sort of person who would enjoy looking at lions and learning something about them. I hope that anyone with an interest in animals will find pleasure or information or even both among the following pages. Such a person might well be a scientist, but need not be; I have tried to give the results of scientific work in a readable form which anyone can understand. You will not find tables of data here, but the bibliography will tell you where to find further information if you want it.

Getting across mere information is relatively easy. I have tried as well to convey something of my approach to lions (in the non-literal sense), of the methods and problems involved in studying them, of the kind of questions to which I tried to find answers, and of the interest and enjoyment inherent in such fascinating work. This last is perhaps the most difficult in print; in my landrover I would have found it much easier to get all this across to you.

I enormously enjoyed the four years I spent studying lions in the Serengeti, and I want to thank everyone who helped to make it possible, fruitful and a pleasure. The trouble is that there are so many people and organizations who contributed in so many different ways. On the financial side, I am indebted to the Natural Environment Research Council (which means also to you as taxpayers) for a research fellowship, then to the Royal Society in London for a travel grant, and to the African Wildlife Leadership Foundation of Washington DC for a research grant. I am most grateful too to the New York Zoological Society who provided a grant for invaluable radio-tracking equipment, and to my parents for a loan to buy my weary landrover (as well as for the innumerable other things over the years, such as producing the author, with which this book is not concerned).

For the privilege of working in the Serengeti I am indebted to the Directors and Trustees of the Tanzania National Parks organization, and to Serengeti park wardens David Babu, Sandy Field, Philip Ole Sayalel, John Stevenson, and Myles Turner for permissions and assistance given even when they did not necessarily agree with 'all this messing about with lions'.

The Serengeti Research Institute was the ideal base for zoological field work.* It provided not only such mundane but helpful facilities as maps, electricity, library, film processing, desk computer, car repairs, equipment and storage space, but also a fine atmosphere of co-operation, stimulation and friendliness among the scientists and their families from seven countries. I am grateful to all of the following for a great variety of kindnesses: reports of lions and their kills, lending spare tyres or *in extremis* cars, advice with calculations, identifying trees, cheetah photographs, help with equipment, discussions, parties and flights, and so on almost endlessly. I hope that Messrs Bradley, Braun, Bunning, Croze, De Wit, Duncan, Gerresheim, Gogan, Gwamaka, Herlocker, Hoeck, Houston, Jarman, Inglis, Kreulen, Kruuk, Kurji, Lamprecht, Lamprey, Mcharo, Mejia, Norton-Griffiths, Pennycuick, Root, Schaller, Schiemann, Sichelwe and Sinclair, and their wives, will appreciate my problems in thanking them all individually, and will accept collectively my gratitude.

However difficult, though, I must single out for special thanks some

* This is Serengeti Research Institute Contribution No. 204.

8

few from among the long list of my creditors. Hugh Lamprey, as Director, enabled me to get to the Serengeti Research Institute in the first place, and gently organized the whole team of scientists working there. Hans Kruuk and Peter Jarman gave me most practical help and advice in the early learning stages of my work. Hans, Colin Pennycuick and Hendrik Hoeck kindly flew me many times over my study area to count animals or look for lost lions; occasional aerial radio-tracking, piloted by Hoeck or by Kruuk, was exceedingly useful. Jack Inglis helped with radio-tracking equipment and arguments about it.

On the more social side, I should like to thank the many wives who kindly provided meals and civilization for a hungry retiring bachelor back from a stint of isolation. The managers of Lobo Wildlife Lodge, the Merchant and Wilks families, assisted similarly. Ian and Shirley Gibson, who had first got me bitten by the Africa bug seven years earlier, acted as kind hosts during my occasional visits to Nairobi. When they left, their place was amply taken by Alasdair and Rosemary Macdonald, who used also sometimes to come down to the Serengeti 'to feed Brian the Lion in his hovel'. On one such visit, they brought, along with other more edible goodies, a stranger called Kate Gillie who is now Kate Bertram; I am most grateful – for all they supplied.

During the writing-up stages after I left the Serengeti, I am indebted to the Sub-Department of Animal Behaviour at Madingley, Cambridge, for providing a base, and to Lilyan White for kindly and typically allowing me space in her room there. Patrick Hamilton and my parents produced useful comments on much of the text of this book. A few of the photographs I did not take myself: I must thank Hendrik Hoeck for numbers 16 and 17, Andrew Laurie for plate 11, John King and the African Wildlife Leadership Foundation for number 15, and an unknown visitor to the Serengeti who kindly sent number 83.

Finally, I am enormously grateful to my wife Kate for a great deal of typing (a real labour of love since her two typing fingers are no faster than mine), for abusing and amending the manuscript, for helping during some very long photograph-printing sessions, and for her patience with the author throughout.

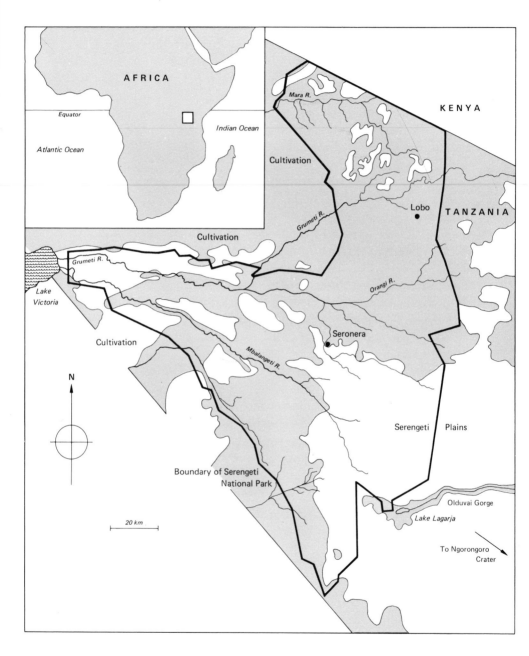

AFRICA

Equator

Atlantic Ocean

Indian Ocean

KENYA

Mara R.

Cultivation

Lobo

TANZANIA

Grumeti R.

Cultivation

Grumeti R.

Orangi R.

Lake
Victoria

Cultivation

Seronera

N

Mbalangeti R.

Serengeti   Plains

Boundary of Serengeti
National Park

Olduvai Gorge

Lake Lagarja

20 km

To Ngorongoro
Crater

10

1 · The Serengeti and its lions

Until recently almost nothing was known about wild lions in their natural environment. Throughout his history, man has thought of them in a variety of curious ways. Many people have looked upon lions as noble and courageous, and have used lion symbols on coats of arms, shields and national flags. Leonine statues are often to be found littered around impressive buildings to make them more so, and it is surely not coincidence that lions in a group were called collectively a 'pride'.

It is not clear just how or why the 'King of Beasts' acquired his title; I suspect it was partly because he was occasionally liable to hunt, kill, and eat people. Man-eating arouses surprisingly deep emotions – although we are carnivorous, we abhor the idea of being eaten ourselves – and people have often imputed spiritual powers to the lions who went in for it.

Other people went in for killing lions. Europeans in pursuit of 'big game' slaughtered thousands of them, and inflated many egos in the process. Cattle owners in Africa tended to look on lions as a particularly powerful, cruel and wasteful kind of vermin against which their cattle had to be protected. Although it is small consolation to the victims, we now know that both man-eating and stock-raiding are aberrant behaviour by a small number of lions in new circumstances brought about by man's introduction of extraordinarily vulnerable prey, including himself. It has only recently become possible to discover this. Previous generations' preoccupation with destroying them made lions timid and difficult to observe. The change in our orientation, and the setting up of national parks in which animals have become accustomed to the presence of humans in vehicles, have now made it possible to observe and study normal lions systematically.

The first full scientific study of lions in the wild was carried out from 1966 to 1969 by George Schaller in the Serengeti National Park in Tanzania. He studied nomadic lions on the open grass plains and two resident prides at the edge of the plains, paying particular attention to their feeding and their effects on prey species. I then studied lions in the Serengeti for a little over four years, from 1969 to 1973, as I describe in this book, and since 1974 David and Jeannette Bygott have been continuing with lion work there.

Lions have been rather little studied elsewhere, the main exceptions being the work of Judith Rudnai for several years in and around Nairobi National Park in Kenya, of G.L. Smuts and his colleagues in the Kruger National Park in South Africa, and of Paul Joslin in the Gir Forest in India on the scarce Asiatic lion.

This book is based, of course, on my own experiences in the Serengeti. I have tried to describe the typical rather than the exceptional, in order to explain the essentials of lions' normal way of life and the factors which shape it. I think the woodlands of the Serengeti are reasonably representative of good lion habitats, in providing resident prey and concealment throughout the year. I realize that the typical lion or the typical habitat is as elusive and as arbitrary as, say, the typical human being; nevertheless, we could easily recognize one which was grossly abnormal. Judging by what has been written of lions elsewhere, they do not differ in major ways from what I and others have found in the Serengeti.

The Serengeti is a superb place to work in or to visit. It is an area of about five thousand square miles, roughly the size of Northern Ireland or the state of Connecticut. About two-thirds of it is woodland, with undulating hills separated by numerous streams or drainage lines. *Acacias* (thorn trees) up to thirty feet high are dotted all over the countryside, in some places very sparsely and in others so close together that it is almost impossible for a vehicle to weave its way through them. The hilltops, slopes and drainage lines have different *Acacia* species growing on them, representing different underlying soil or drainage conditions, while along the larger and more nearly permanent streams grow much bigger trees, figs being some of the most notable.

Everywhere underfoot is grass, though rarely looking soft, green or meadowlike. During the wet season, which usually lasts from December to May, the grass grows to a height of three feet or more, topped by spiky seed heads. It dries as the wet season fades away, taking its nutrients down into the roots and turning a diluted gold

12

1 A cub of about four months, showing the disproportionately large ears of young lions

2 A very few of the migratory zebras and wildebeest which provide the Serengeti lions' main food

colour. During the dry season this coarse and scarcely edible hay is consumed by grass fires or by hungry herbivores who also trample and flatten it. The minerals from the grass are returned to the soil – via ash, via herbivore dung and the dung beetles which feed on it, or via the termites which consume any dead plant material – to produce rapid new growth when the next rainy season comes.

New grass provides the food for most of the hoofed animals for which the Serengeti is famous. Between 10 and 20 per cent of these animals – the buffaloes, warthogs, impalas, hartebeests, waterbucks and several other small antelopes – belong to resident species, remaining in the same area throughout the year, feeding on what grass they can find there. Five other species have adopted the different strategy of being nomadic and migrating to where food is available, and these are the most abundant species in the area: about a million wildebeest (also known as gnus), perhaps half as many gazelles (Thomson's and Grant's), about a third as many zebras and some seven thousand elands. These migratory animals move out south-east onto the huge open grass plains which make up the remaining third of the national park, when the first rain there makes the volcanic soil sprout with new and nutritive short green grass. The dry season comes earliest to the plains, pushing the migratory species back into the woodlands where the grass grows higher and lasts for longer. When on the plains, the migrants are preyed upon by nomadic lions, by the abundant hyaenas, and by the scarce cheetahs and wild dogs; in the woodlands their commonest predators are lions and leopards. The woodlands are the home, too, of the browsers – animals which eat shrubs and trees rather than grasses. Giraffes are by far the commonest of these, rhinos the rarest, and elephants the species which has the most noticeable impact on these woodlands by pushing over or de-barking large trees. Woodland country is necessary too for the tsetse flies which, by carrying sleeping sickness, have been primarily responsible for the Serengeti remaining uninhabited by humans and their cattle. Even outside the park boundaries the country is still only sparsely settled, and wild animals roam freely in and out of the park.

The Serengeti has many features to justify its fine reputation: the wonderful sense of space on the open expanse of the plains; the spectacle of the herds of hundreds of thousands of wildebeest grazing, or the endless winding strings of galloping gnu after galloping gnu; the abundance and observability of the large predator species; and the tremendous variety of the mammal and bird fauna. In addition, as the late Sir

Julian Huxley observed, another of the park's distinctions is in having a fine wildlife research unit, unrivalled in Africa at least. The Serengeti Research Institute, under the direction of the Tanzania National Parks organization, was established in 1966, with two main objectives: to discover as much as possible of the ecology of the area, and to provide information which would be of use to the park management authorities. I was fortunate enough to be able to join the Institute in August 1969, as the resident lionologist, with the task of discovering what I could about the relatively unknown lions inhabiting the woodlands.

There is no need to describe my subjects in much detail, because most people have a fair idea of what lions look like – enormous cats. They have a typically catlike body, and their eyes are similarly adapted to seeing at night. Their short, sharp curved claws can be retracted into sheaths in the paws when the lion is walking, so preventing them from getting blunted. The teeth show adaptations to a predatory way of life. The powerful canine teeth are long and sharply pointed, suitable both for holding prey and for fighting; the molar teeth behind are adapted to slicing through pieces of meat.

The fur is mainly sandy or tawny in colour (what *is* tawn?), but not uniformly so. On the belly and inside the legs it is much softer, longer and whiter; the last is a standard camouflaging technique for concealing a solid object by reducing the darkness of its shaded parts. Seen at

3 A cub of a little over a year attempts to rest comfortably on the skeleton of a fallen tree

night by starlight, if you *can* see them, lions appear almost uniformly grey and superbly ghostlike, an impression heightened by their very silent movement. They drift or flit noiselessly, the soft pads on their paws enabling them to walk soundlessly but on the other hand making them vulnerable to thorns. By day, the colour of their coat beautifully matches that of sun-dried grass stems, a matching which is largely wasted because the grass is often green and in any case it is doubtful whether either lions or their prey can see much in colour. The backs of the round, not pointed, ears are black, in marked contrast to the whole of the rest of the body except the tail tuft. Lions are unique among cats in having a tuft of long hair, black in colour, at the end of the tail, for most cats' tails are uniformly furred all along their length. It is often stated that this tail tuft contains a spur with which the lion is supposed to lash his flanks to fuel his anger; but in fact he doesn't do so, and in any case none of the lions' tails I examined had a noticeably sharp end.

Lions are unique among cats in another more notable way, namely that the male has a mane. The hair round the back of the head and on the neck and shoulders of an adult male grows up to six inches long, sticks outwards and is darker in colour than the rest of his fur, making him look both more impressive than a female and much larger. He is in any case considerably larger than she. Average adult males I weighed were about 420 lb, or 30 stone, about one-and-a-half times as much as a lioness. A male is more solidly built and larger in all directions, standing 3-3½ feet high at the shoulder, with a chest girth of about 4 feet, and a total body length from nose to tail tip of around 9 feet. Measurements of record-sized lions in the past have always been taken from shot animals or from their skins, both of which can be stretched out more than is possible with a live lion, for hunters, like fishermen, want their victims to have been large. I found that even live (immobilized) lions were awkwardly stretchable and almost impossible to measure reliably except around the chest.

The Serengeti contains about two thousand lions. They are the largest of the predators there, and one of the most social. We must remember, though, that they form only one thread in the whole complicated web of animal and plant life in the area. This book concentrates on lions and on their social life because my job and my interests coincided neatly on this topic. Yet a biologist would have to be mentally blinkered not to be intrigued too by the many other fascinating threads all around him, always producing something to admire, puzzle over and remember.

16

My memories of a fascinating four years spent studying lions in the Serengeti are, of course, all jumbled together, with the highlights and hitches remaining most vivid against a background of interest and enjoyment. I shall always remember the Serengeti's incredible variety of animals, of all manner of shapes, sizes and colours, from black buffaloes to brilliant coloured beetles, sunbirds to serval cats, leopards, elephants, tortoises and tsetse flies. At the same time I shall remember the literally thousands of painful bites I received from those innumerable and infuriating tsetse flies, and the hair-raising chases when on several occasions herds of irate elephants pursued me in my ailing landrover zigzagging its way among the thorn trees as I tried to escape.

4 An adult male. Note the large mane which increases the apparent size of his head, and the scars on his nose which provided me with a useful means of recognizing him

5 A lioness at rest with two cubs of roughly a year old. Only the left-hand one is hers

I shall never forget the wonderful feeling of space and timelessness as I looked from the top of a rock over hundreds of square miles of unspoilt empty country – and nor will I forget the time spent in changing or repairing heavy tyres punctured at the rate of two or three a week by the ubiquitous thorns. When the massive wildebeest herds were migrating through my study area, their beautiful long winding migrating lines, their chaotic dense milling congregation and the gentle continuous mooing of the multitude made me forget that for three weeks afterwards the area would be infested with the maddening little flies which breed in wildebeest droppings and apparently spend the rest of their lives crawling over scientists' faces!

The climate was superb. In the dry season, the strong breeze from the south-east kept the humidity down and the air invigorating despite the temperature; it also seized and hurled along the dust thrown up by car tyres, making driving downwind a choking and often unseeing occupation. In the dry season, too, the stems of the dried-out hibiscus plants shed a glistening cascade of skin-irritating hairs as I drove among them, and I would forget that only a few months earlier in the rainy season I had rejoiced in the beautiful purple flowers of these same hibiscus, set against the delicate orange wild gladioli and a whole range of smaller flowers. The wet season induced many birds to don their dazzling breeding plumage, brought birds and frogs into song, and made the whole country sprout rich and green. It also made the grass grow so high that I could not see the hidden rocks or warthog holes onto or into which I was slowly and blindly driving; it made the streams treacherously difficult to cross without getting stuck; and it made active the slugs which crawled into my hovel and devoured the labels on my tins of food so I could never plan what I was going to eat (except that square tins were usually meat!).

The lions too provided a wide variety of experiences. The satisfaction at the end of a smooth and successful lion-darting and radio-collaring operation (Chapter 2) would be counterbalanced by the maddening and slowly growing realization some weeks later that the radio had packed up prematurely. Knowing the life histories of many lions and following their fluctuating fortunes was intriguing, predicting what would happen to them a fascinating pastime. I had plenty of time for

6 A pair of lions rest beside a pool; the fact that they are so close together is an indication that the lioness is in oestrus

such pastimes during the many very long, very hot hours when the lions were dozing peacefully in the only small cool patch of shade and I was outside it, roasting uncomfortably in an overheated landrover, watching them do nothing. But then the unpredictability and exhilaration of their occasional hunting attempts would make the long and tedious wait worth while. I shall not forget the miles of driving a rattling car over what felt like hot corrugated concrete fields, fruitlessly searching for lions which seemed to be either transparent or subterranean; nor shall I forget the frustration of tracking down a radio signal for three hours through a rainy windy night and through thorn trees and painfully over rocks and holes, only to find that the lion had concealed itself in a thicket or inaccessible river bed. Yet later the sight of golden lions in golden grass in golden early morning sunlight more than compensated for such tribulations. And there can be few more idyllic moments than when, lying awake in a small car in the bright light of the full equatorial moon, I would hear the very soft scrunch of paws on the ground beside the car, followed by the tremendously powerful and majestic roar of a male lion nearby proclaiming his ownership of the land which returned the echoes of his thundering.

2 · Studying lions

Before I went to the Serengeti I knew very little about lions. There were many anecdotal and often conflicting accounts of the way lions lived in the wild, and of course some famous descriptions of individual hand-reared or circus lions, but at that time there was almost no published scientific information. In any case, I had been occupied previously with studying mynah birds in India. I quickly read up as much as I could about my new subjects, and realized that few other people knew much either.

The scientific name for the lion species is *Panthera leo*. Linnaeus, the founder of the international classification system for animals and plants, used the name *Felis leo*, seeing the many similarities between lions and the domestic cat, *Felis domesticus*. Later taxonomists, however, saw what they considered basic differences between the large cats and the small ones, and consequently put lions, tigers, leopards and jaguars into the genus *Panthera*. These large cat species can sometimes be persuaded to interbreed in captivity, producing ligers and tigons, leopons, leopard-jaguar crosses and so on. Similarly, some of the two dozen or so small cat species have been made to interbreed without great difficulty. It is possible that the lack of hybrids between big and small cats is due partly to physiological incompatibility, but I think there is also the powerful practical reason that if they were put together the big cat would probably eat the small cat at once rather than mate with it!

Lions from different parts of their geographical range have been allocated to different subspecies. The validity of this is rather dubious since it is based mainly on small numbers of skins, and characteristics such as coat and mane colour varied considerably even within the

7 A pair of lions rests together out in the sun during a mating period

single population I was studying. The Serengeti lion, with which this book is mainly concerned, belongs to the subspecies *Panthera leo massaicus*, the Masai lion, but I doubt whether it is radically different from any other lion subspecies.

While on terminology, I should make clear one or two other points. Lions share with man and dogs the dubious distinction that the species' name is the same as that of the *male* of the species. (We do not refer to these species of animals as lionesses, women or bitches. By contrast, with some of the more productive species of animals, we do just that. We often use the words goose, duck, hen and cow to mean the species as a whole and have special terms – gander, drake, cock and bull – for the male of that species.) To avoid confusion, whenever I use the word 'lion' I mean a member of the lion species, of either sex. I use 'male' or 'female' to indicate the sex; I also use the word 'lioness' for a female, but 'lion' does not mean a male. Nor is 'lion' plural. Prevalent in Africa, and probably a leftover from the 'big game' era is the use of the species name in the plural without a final 's' – as in 'I bagged seven lion' or 'leopard have spots'. This can sometimes be confusing and since it does not seem necessary I talk of lions, leopards and cheetahs if there are more than one of them

My study of lions in the Serengeti was in two parts. At Lobo, a

8 The ten-foot-square corrugated iron hovel in which I lived. It was not as gloomy as it looks, for there was a small window at each side

wooded region in the north-east of the park, I investigated particularly how many lions there were, what controlled their numbers, how they moved in relation to their food supply, what they were feeding upon, and what effect their predation had on their prey species. I spent about two-thirds of my time there, up to a fortnight at a stretch, living alone in a ten-foot-square corrugated iron hovel concealed under a bush, a dwelling which was partly responsible for earning me the nickname of

23

the 'Lobo Hobo'. The rest of the time I spent at the Serengeti Research Institute near Seronera, in the centre of the park. Here, apart from getting washed and civilized, having my sick car temporarily cured, and constructing radio-collars and working on data, I made intermittent observations on the two large prides in the tourist area which Schaller had studied. I established a system of keeping long-term records of the life histories and reproduction of all the known individuals in these prides, and passed on these records to my successors. Thus we now have twelve years of breeding records for some two dozen wild lions. There are very few other individual wild animals anywhere in the world which have been documented for so long.

FINDING LIONS

Just finding lions to observe was the first problem, and more of a problem than one might at first think. After all, with only about two thousand lions in the five thousand square miles of the Serengeti, the average area to be thoroughly searched to find a group of four lions is some ten square miles, and doing this takes an awful lot of time. To make matters worse, lions do not necessarily make themselves conspicuous, and indeed they may conceal themselves in patches of long grass, thickets, or deep overgrown river courses. The chances of finding them were better if I started early in the day, for in the cool couple of hours after dawn lions are often still out in the open, and the low sun makes their flanks glow golden. Lions are also likely to be active at that time of day, and a moving object is much easier to detect than a motionless one. An hour's searching at dawn was worth at least three hours' searching later.

As well as actually looking for lions, I always paid attention to sounds or signs of them. Lions sometimes roar early in the morning, and thus might unwittingly lead me to the source of the noise. Seeing fresh footprints or droppings, too, would often give an indication that there were lions nearby and possibly in which direction they were to be found. Some people can tell that there are lions nearby by smelling them, but this is something which I never managed to do.

I would not be the only animal looking for lions: potential victims have to keep on the lookout for them too. If a wildebeest sees a lion it makes sure it cannot be ambushed, snorts loudly and watches the predator intently. A hundred pairs of eyes were better than my one pair

9 The alert upright posture of two giraffes watching a predator. Their size makes them excellent lion-indicators, because of their high vantage point and their conspicuousness: they can easily see the lion, and I can easily see them

alone, and by listening for the sharp alarm snorts of ungulates (hoofed animals) I sometimes found lions which I would otherwise have missed. Even a silent ungulate's posture as it keeps an eye on the predator can be revealing, particularly in the case of giraffes which can both see and be seen from such a long distance away. Other species do different things. Jackals, for example, often approach to within quite close range of the lion and bark at it incessantly with repeated shrill squeaky yaps. The sound of jackals barking was worth investigating, even though it often led to nothing but another jackal. The behaviour of buffalo bulls also sometimes indicated the presence of a lion group. Usually they ignored my landrover when it was far away, but fled if it came within about forty yards of them. But if there were lions nearby, the buffaloes would often threaten or very occasionally charge my vehicle; presumably the attentions or smell of the lions had made them more tense or aggressive.

Vultures were a much better clue. A group of these large dark birds on the branches of a tree very often indicated that there was both a carcass and a predator below. Lions guard their kills, and prevent

10 A gathering of vultures in a fever tree. Their presence there indicates a meal which they cannot yet get at, often because there are lions still feeding. Many times I found lions by finding vultures which had found lion kills first

vultures and other scavengers from feeding. Then, when the lions leave, the vultures which have been waiting patiently for hours descend from their trees, converge on the remains of the carcass and quickly remove any edible portions. Vultures feeding on the ground, however, do not indicate lions: they indicate a food source for the vultures without a predator in attendance; and since many more animals die of natural causes than through being caught by lions it is unlikely that a lion is nearby. But although unlikely, it was worth looking near such vulture-covered carcasses in case there should be a lion just departing. The sight of a tall circling stack of vultures was no guide either; if they were circling it was because they wanted to go up, which meant that there was no food left, and the predator, even if there had been one, had long since departed. (When vultures want to go up, they wait for a thermal upcurrent to soar in, watching the clouds and other vultures to find out where there is such an upcurrent.)

Despite these clues, which were themselves not abundant, lions were still not easy to find, and I spent a great deal of time driving slowly and unsuccessfully through the countryside, stopping to scan all around with binoculars from the car roof or the top of a rock outcrop or 'kopje' as they are called. With practice I got much better at detecting the flick of a lion's ear in long grass, at noticing a hartebeest's unusually upright alert posture, at learning which particular places lions were likely to visit, and at distinguishing under the shade of a very distant tree which dark lumps could not be rocks, termite mounds, fallen branches, warthogs or any of the other objects which so inconveniently rest in shady patches to imitate lions and to frustrate lionologists.

I also used two other techniques for finding lions. In tourist areas it was always worth keeping an eye out for a cluster of stationary tourist minibuses (minibi?), for *Homo sapiens* on holiday is keen to watch and photograph lions, leopards or cheetahs, and spends much more time near them than near other species. But this could work only in areas where there were many tourists, and it had at least three drawbacks. Tourists did not get up early enough in the morning, the lions they found tended to be ones which were relatively easy to find anyway, and with several vehicles often too close to them the lions were disturbed and did even less than they otherwise would. The other technique I used for finding lions, and one which was more valuable than all the others put together, was radio-tracking them – making the lion wear a collar containing a radio-transmitter which I could find whenever I wanted. Later in this chapter I shall describe how I did this.

27

Having at last found a group of lions, my first task was always to determine who all the individuals were. I did not want to mark the lions I was studying, and in any case this was not necessary because all lions are different, if looked at carefully enough. Lions themselves are clearly able to recognize and distinguish between different individuals, and so can humans with practice. I could recognize over two hundred different adult lions in my woodland study area at Lobo, the limit being set by the number of lions living within the area. I used several methods to do so.

By a first quick classification I would put each lion into one of several obvious categories: whether it was male or female, and whether cub, subadult, adult or old. I would then look for particular characteristics of that animal. Some lions have very clear features by which it is possible to recognize them, usually the results of injuries. For example, a number of lions lose the tuft on the tip of their tail, and a few even the whole tail, enabling me at once to narrow down enormously the number of possible animals it could be. Some are blind in one eye, which is another very useful clue to their identity.

In the course of their lives, lions acquire nicks in their ears, presumably in a number of different ways, such as on thorns, in fights and while making kills, but one of the commonest causes appears to be when a group is feeding at a kill. A considerable amount of squabbling takes place as lions feed, and they push and scratch one another with their paws and claws. It seemed that on average lions tended to have their left ear more damaged than their right ear, and the reason for this became clear when I watched them struggling at kills. Most of them appeared to be slightly right-handed, using their right paw more often than their left to swat at competitors, and as a lion, if you use your right paw you are more likely to connect with the left ear of an adversary. Nicks in the ears stay permanently and may become bigger with time because of biting flies and because a nick provides a weak point for further tearing. As a way of recognizing individual lions, ear irregularities were a good first method, provided I bore in mind the possibility of a new nick having appeared in a lion's ear since I had last seen the animal. The method was especially useful with older lions, who had had more time to acquire injuries to their ears. Some ears were particularly 'good' (from my point of view!) in having huge notches, folding down, or even being absent altogether.

28

The teeth provided another good way of distinguishing one lion from another. The large canine teeth change with age, as described later, and they may also get broken. The small incisor teeth have all disappeared in a very old lion, and even quite a young animal frequently has one or more of them missing. The position of the gap or gaps can vary greatly: after all, there are sixty-three different possible combinations by which between one and all six of a lion's lower incisor teeth can be missing. As with ear defects, however, one must remember that although a tooth once lost is not replaced, a tooth can have disappeared since one last saw that individual. It is in fact much easier to see a lion's teeth than it sounds. When resting on a hot day, lions frequently lie with their mouths open, panting lightly. I could see their lower front teeth then, and also when they were beginning to become active and so yawning frequently. (Incidentally, yawning seems to be contagious among lions, as it is among humans: when one lion yawns, another is likely to do so. It is also contagious from lion to man, and a group waking up made me yawn too, but it was not contagious in reverse, and I never succeeded in making a lion yawn, so that I could see its teeth, by yawning at it.)

Scars were often useful labels, too. Lions get many small injuries in fights, squabbles and hunts, and some of these scars remain. On most of the body they become overgrown with the fur and cease to be visible unless they are very large, but on the face even quite small scars may be permanent. One cannot tell if a new injury will leave a 'nice' permanent scar, but a scar on the nose which has lasted for, say, a year will probably last for ever. Again one has to bear in mind that new scars can appear between successive sightings of the same individual.

Whisker spots can also provide a useful means of recognition. Lions have large whiskers, arranged in parallel horizontal rows along the cheeks, a small dark spot marking the place where each whisker emerges. In the top row there are no actual whiskers, but only a few spots. The position of these few spots in relation to the whisker spots in the row below varies from lion to lion, and also between the two sides of the face of the same animal. Colin Pennycuick and Judith Rudnai found that this was a useful method of recognizing individual lions in the Nairobi National Park, and showed that if the population was relatively small there was little chance of two different lions having the same arrangement of whisker spots. In a large population such as mine in the Serengeti this did not hold, and I had a number of cases of different individuals having identical whisker spot patterns. Nonethe-

11 a&b The left and right sides of the face of a four-year-old male. Note that the pattern of whisker spots is different on the two sides of the face

less, these spots provided yet one more way in which lions usually differ from one another, and I found them useful in conjunction with other methods of recognizing individuals. They were particularly helpful with cubs and young animals which had not yet acquired nicks in their ears or other blemishes and so were difficult to distinguish by other means, and also when comparing photographs. The disadvantages were that I had to be relatively close to the lion before I could see the position of the whisker spots clearly enough, and also that the angle at which I was looking at the lion often made it difficult to determine exactly the position of the spots.

Some lions were much more difficult to recognize than others, and they were sometimes most easily distinguishable by the fact that they were always or often in the company of another which was easily recognizable. I had to be careful with this approach, for I might have been confusing two similar individuals, but the presence of the easily recognizable animal could often narrow down the number of lions which needed to be considered closely.

We recognize many different humans, yet we do not pay attention to nicks in their ears, scars, teeth or whiskers. Their faces just look different. So do lions' faces. Practice helps: just as it is only at first that 'all Chinese look alike', so a lion observer learns what features are worth looking at in detail, and begins to recognize and remember these features, excluding the unhelpful ones. (By analogy, Europeans tend to pay much attention to human hair colour, which varies greatly among different individuals. Indians, whose hair colour varies much less than their complexions, seem to pay far more attention to complexion in describing and recognizing people.) The better I got to know lions, and individual lions especially, the more it became possible to identify them by their general appearance, rather than by particular characteristics; a quick glance at the face told me which lion I was looking at.

However well one knows a lion, though, it is always useful to have a tangible means of identification, for one's memory of a lion's appearance can change, as can the lion to some extent if a long period elapses during which it is not seen. I made an identity card for each animal, with a caricature of the face of a lion, onto which I could mark any nicks in the outline of the ears, could show whisker spots and their relative positions, and could indicate any scars and spots on the muzzle. I left space at the side for a description of the lion's general appearance, of its teeth, and of other notable features elsewhere on its body. On the back of the card I stuck black and white photographs of the two sides of the

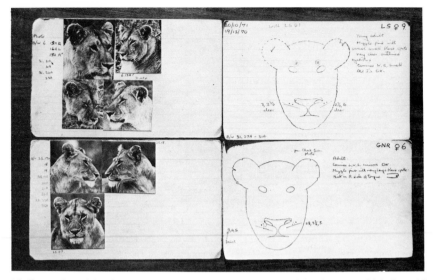

12 Four of my identity cards for lions. Note the outline of the face on which I could show distinguishing features, and photographs on the reverse side

lion's face. My set of cards went everywhere with me in the landrover, and after four years was tattered, grubby and invaluable.

I gave each animal an identifying code and number. Names would have been easier to remember, but I did not give my lions names for two reasons. First, it is difficult to find completely neutral names without connotations which might bias what I recorded or observed. Second, and more important, it could be quite valuable to be unable to remember the lion's label easily. I might see a lioness who I knew perfectly well was 'that one with the two nicks in her left ear and a scar below her right eye', but since I could not remember if she was GR 17 or GR 18, I had to look at my identity cards. This was a thoroughly good thing for it helped to prevent undetected, and therefore perpetuated, mis-identifications, and drew my attention to any changes in that individual's appearance since the last time I had seen her.

The letters GR stood for Grumeti River. Other codes were LS for Lobo Stream, BC for Brian's Crossing (an apparently unpromising place where I managed to coax my car across a stream), PL for Poachers' Lookout, SK for Stinking Kopje ('stinking' because a baboon troop always defaecated there), NP for Nowhere Particular (a large featureless area), WD for With Dykes (visiting friends), EK for Eland Kill, and suchlike. When I first encountered an unknown lioness, for example, I

32

gave her a label (such as SK Female 1) according to where or in what circumstances I saw her. Then any other lions which I subsequently saw with that animal received labels with the same code, SK Females 2, 3, 4, and so on – duller, perhaps, but I think preferable to names such as Agatha or Zachariah.

WATCHING LIONS

How easily a lion could be recognized depended partly on how close I could get to it. All my observations were made from a landrover, not for the reasons one might think but because lions in the wild are afraid of humans on foot. If I were to get out of the car when in sight of a group of lions they would become nervous and make off. When I first started work in my study area at Lobo, the lions there were afraid of vehicles too, and would sometimes flee when my car appeared a couple of hundred yards away from them. To get close to them I would drive slowly and steadily, but at an angle towards rather than straight towards them. If the lions showed signs of unease or restlessness I switched off the engine at once and waited for several minutes until they got used to my presence and relaxed; then I started to approach again. Fortunately lions are reluctant to leave a patch of shade unless they have to, and although it might take a couple of hours to do so, I could usually get to within thirty yards of any group of lions I found. With time some of them became thoroughly habituated, like lions in most tourist areas, and allowed vehicles to drive straight up to within twenty yards of them.

I watched them with binoculars and made notes on what was going on. With the help of my identity cards I identified all the individuals there, making new cards for any new animals and taking photographs of any animals of whom I had not already got good portraits. I noted where they were, what type of vegetation they were in, and what they were doing. Usually they were all lying inactive, in which case I recorded where they lay in relation to one another. If it was early or late in the day they were more likely to be behaving in an interesting way – greeting, grooming or playing with one another – in which case I recorded who did what to whom. I observed and noted any individuals who were mating, clearly pregnant, lactating, or suckling cubs, and I watched from a distance any hunting attempts which took place.

I was interested also in the food intake and ageing of my subjects. I developed a rough way of recording how much food there was in each lion's stomach each time I saw it. A lion can eat at one 'sitting' a

13 a&b An elderly male lion, his age showing in the wear on his canine teeth, both of which are broken and worn short. By comparison, a young lioness yawning shows her rough tongue, her teeth and her youth – her canines are long, sharp and white, and she has her full complement of incisor teeth in each jaw

quantity of meat up to about 20 per cent of its own weight. This is comparable to an average man eating about forty-five large steaks at one meal and not surprisingly it shows. A full lion has a greatly swollen and distended belly, and I used a rough visual scale to estimate how swollen, ranging from 1 (bloated) to 6 (starving).

I could tell the approximate age of any lion up to about three years old by its size. After that it became more difficult to age them, but one way which was helpful with younger adults was by using the muzzle, which is pink in cubs and black in old adults. The blackening occurs by the development of several small black pigment spots at different points on the muzzle; these gradually grow and merge with one another. The extent of the blackening could indicate the relative age of the lion, and the positions of the few early black spots could also be another useful way of telling different lions apart.

The teeth, too, gave a measure of a lion's age, and were particularly useful with older lions. The canine teeth, which are long, sharp and creamy white in young adults, gradually become blunted and broken off short with age, and they change first to a yellowish colour and then to almost a toffee brown. At the same time the incisor teeth are progressively lost. Again these changes helped me both to age a lion and to recognize each one individually.

RADIO-TRACKING LIONS

The methods of finding lions which I have already described were time-consuming, and did not enable me to find a particular lion when I wanted to, something which was important for my study. I therefore decided to resort to radio-tracking, a method which had been used with several species but never before with numbers of lions or for more than a few days. The principle is to make the lion wear a radio-collar, containing a small transmitter, batteries to power it and twelve inches of aerial. In the Research Institute's workshop I connected these components together, sealed them inside a block of dental acrylic material – the hard plastic of which the plates for false teeth are made – and connected each end of the block to a length of tough machine belting. Later I would bolt the ends of this together round the neck of an immobilized lion, each collar thus being individually tailored to its wearer. It was important to get the size right – not so tight that it constricted the neck, nor so loose that it could swing about freely or even slip off over the head.

To fit a collar I would immobilize the lion by injecting it with a suitable drug, using a dart from a dart gun. With practice and care this was a straightforward operation, which I often used to carry out alone. I wanted to be able to observe lions behaving normally afterwards, and therefore one of my main considerations was to avoid all disturbance both to the darted lion and to its companions.

Which lion I chose to radio-collar depended on what sort of information I was hoping to obtain, which pride I wanted to keep track of, and so on. Once I had decided on the recipient, it sometimes took many days before I managed to find it. Then, having done so, the next problem was to get close enough to it. I would approach even more slowly and obliquely than usual, stopping the car at once if the lion seemed at all uneasy. I had to get to within about twenty-five yards, and preferably much closer, before firing a dart at a lion because dart guns are inaccurate and I could not afford to miss or mis-hit. The dart consists of an aluminium tube with a hollow needle at one end and a tuft of wool at the other to act as a tail; inside is a rubber plunger, in front of which is placed the drug in solution, while behind the plunger is a very small explosive charge. This charge is detonated by the impact of the dart hitting the animal, the rubber plunger is pushed forward, and the drug is forced through the hollow needle into the lion. All this equipment, needed to transport and inject just a few milligrams of drug, is heavy and would injure a soft-skinned animal if the dart were travelling at speed, so it must be fired only slowly, which reduces both its range and its accuracy.

The dart gun I had the use of was quite an elderly one which had been pointed at a large number of animals in its time. Compressed carbon dioxide propelled the dart: two of the sparklets which are sold commercially for putting fizziness into soda water siphons would allow about a dozen darts to be fired, although the later shots scarcely plopped out of the barrel. On one occasion a very weakly propelled dart dropped way below a resting lion's shoulder but by extraordinary chance hit a hind toe and successfully injected the drug into it. With love and practice the gun was usually reliable, and had the great advantage of being almost silent – lions noticed its quiet 'phut' but were not disturbed by it.

Accuracy at first shot was essential. The dart had to strike a muscle block at right angles to its line of flight for the injection mechanism to work, and the receiving lion would rarely allow me a second attempt. I usually aimed at the shoulder muscle because this area provided a

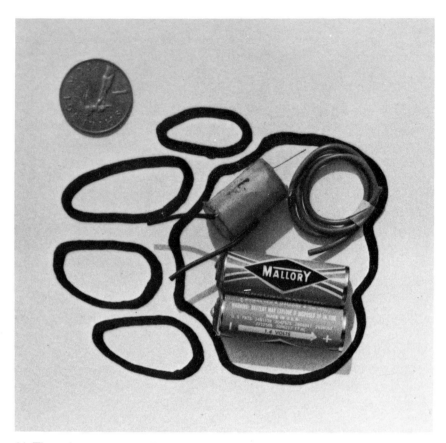

14 The active components of a lion's radio-collar (transmitter, batteries and aerial) are small enough to fit within the outline of a lion's footprint

larger target at right angles on a resting lion, and the lion could not reach, pull out and destroy a dart in its shoulder.

When a lion was darted it normally jumped to its feet with a snort of surprise, thereby also surprising its companions. It trotted or walked a few yards and, for no apparent reason, often picked up a stick and chewed it. It then turned and tried to bite the dart; usually it could not reach it but kept turning in tight circles while trying to do so. Its companions often gathered around the lion at this curious behaviour, and frequently one of them would pull out the dart and chew it. The whole group would then drift off to a nearby patch of shade and relax there, sometimes greeting or grooming the by now partly drugged lion if it continued to behave oddly. After about ten minutes the drug should have taken effect completely and if so the lion would be lying peacefully, unable to raise its head. I could then push the other lions away gently by driving the car slowly straight towards them. A hundred yards would be enough, and from there they often watched me working on their prostrate companion but did not, fortunately, attempt to come back and interfere in my future or in the progress of science.

Sometimes the dose injected was not quite sufficient, because of only partial injection or inaccuracy in estimating the lion's weight, or because I naturally tried to give the lion as little drug as possible so as not to endanger its life nor to have it immobilized for too long a time. In addition, individuals turned out to differ in their reactions to the new and excellent drug (called CI-744, manufactured by Parke Davis) which I was using. Females needed higher doses per kilogramme than males, and timid or disturbed animals more than tame placid ones. An under-dosed lion would snarl and struggle when I came close to it; rather than fire another dart at it, I would approach it quietly from behind and inject a further dose by hand into its backside.

A fully immobilized lion lay relaxed and looking deceptively as though it were asleep, although most of its reflexes were still present. It might lick its lips, flick an ear or sneeze, which could be disconcerting, but it was unconscious and could not notice such indignities as my dragging it into the shade by its hind legs. It would not remember

15 After darting her, I drag an immobilized lioness towards the shade. Her tense foreleg and expression show that she is not yet fully anaesthetized

16 While a lioness lies immobilized, I fit a radio-collar around her neck

17 Demonstrating how completely immobilized a lion can be, I lie beside a newly-collared but not-yet-recovered lioness

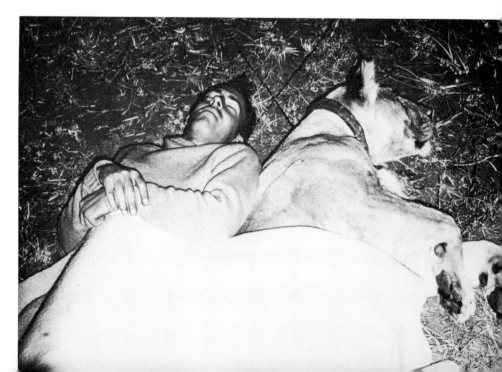

anyway, since the drug causes loss of memory of events around the half hour or so of complete anaesthesia. During this time I would remove the dart if no lion had already done so; fit a radio-collar and test that it was working reasonably; weigh the lion on a hastily assembled platform balanced on two pairs of bathroom scales; take measurements of the still unconscious lion's body, limbs and teeth; examine it for general condition and external parasites; and keep watch on its body temperature and respiration rate to make sure it was not overheating, swabbing its belly with cold water if it was. It was a busy time, and I frequently

18 A male rests under a tree beside the remains of his last meal and the radio-collared lioness who captured it. Tracking the lioness enabled me to find him and to gather data on lions' feeding

forgot to keep an eye open for other lions returning. However, the only lion who ever tried at all determinedly to return was a male whose oestrous female I had immobilized: he made loud mock charges forty yards away, but fortunately his deeply ingrained fear of people was stronger than his sex urge.

After fifteen to fifty minutes, depending on the dose and the individual, the lion would begin to come round, first being able to lift its head just off the ground, and later straining unsteadily to regain its normal posture on its chest. A couple of hours would be needed before the lion could crawl or walk unsteadily away. During this time I would watch it from inside my car, about thirty yards away, far enough so as not to alarm it, but close enough to be able to protect the slowly recovering

creature from attack by any buffaloes, hyaenas or strange lions which might come across it. The process of recovery was usually gradual and smooth; not invariably, though, and I had one particularly anxious and embarrassing moment when I was chased about thirty yards by an immobilized lioness who recovered with astonishing abruptness when I walked over to check that she was not still too deeply anaesthetized. I do not know if I really ran faster than she, but I got back to my car first!

It was most encouraging that darting a lion, if done carefully, did not make it more timid later. The dartèd animal seemed quite unconscious of what had been done to it, while its companions did not see me out of the car at close range. All the lions subsequently became much more accustomed to, and unafraid of, my frequent visits to the group – a group which I should have been unable to find except by homing in on the radio-collar which one of its members was wearing. When the lions recovered from the drug they took almost no notice of the radio-collar. They might shake their head more often than usual for the first few days, or scratch their neck with a hind paw, but they made no attempt whatever to remove the collar, either with their forepaws or on project-ing objects. The collars did not appear to inconvenience the animals in any way: they did not project out sideways or get tangled with vegeta-tion, nor did they rub away the hair on the lion's neck at all. A radio-collar weighs less than 1 per cent of a lion's weight; unless you are reading this book in the bath or in bed you are carrying a proportion-ately much greater weight of clothing without noticing it.

Although the owner of the collar did not object or try to remove it, occasionally other lions did. In the course of grooming a companion's neck, a lion would sometimes encounter the radio-collar, lick it and then try to bite it off. The groomer would be unable to get its shearing carnassial teeth into contact with the collar, and so would pull at it instead, until soon prevented by the snarls of protest from the wearer.

Throughout the four to nine months that its batteries lasted in practice, the transmitter sent out a continuous stream of radio signals. I could detect these with a small receiver and a directional aerial which was portable, if somewhat cumbersome to carry among bushes. From high points – the tops of rock outcrops, or standing on the car roof – I would turn the aerial until I heard a faint signal from the receiver. I would know which radio-collared lion I was detecting because they all had different frequencies, or different 'bleep-rates' if on the same frequency. The range obtainable varied enormously. If the lion was up

42

a tree, a regrettably infrequent occurrence in the Serengeti, the signals could be detected from several miles away. If the lion was sitting on flat ground, I used to get a range of about one-and-a-half miles, while if it was lying down in a hollow the range was very poor.

Radio-tracking lions meant that I could almost guarantee to find particular individuals whenever I wanted to. I found that to safeguard against the collars breaking or packing up prematurely, it was worthwhile to put radio-collars onto two animals in each pride, so that when the signals from one ceased I would be able in time to rediscover that individual via its collared companion. I did not want merely to determine the location of each animal, but to see what it was doing or feeding on, who it was with, and so on. Therefore I did not try to put radio-collars onto a great many animals. Eight lions and two leopards was the maximum number I could manage to track and observe each day. With some individuals I made observations every three hours for several days at a time. Alone, I could not observe them continuously for long periods; in any case at night it was almost impossible to follow lions in the irregular wooded country of my study area, and completely impossible to observe them then without interfering with their hunting. But by finding them at three-hour intervals day and night I could discover where those lions had gone, what they were doing and what kills they had made. I would then drive away to look for other lions if it was still daytime, or, at night, to snatch some sleep in the cramped landrover until the next observation was due. With the help of a vigorous alarm clock, and barring major mishaps, I could keep up these regular observations for up to a week at a stretch until fatigue made me too bad tempered.

LIONS' FEEDING

To discover what the lions were feeding on I had to find them at their kills. Spotting congregations of vultures and radio-tracking individual lions were the most successful methods of doing so, but even with these aids I rarely found more than one or two kills a day. It was difficult to examine a carcass while lions were still present. If I had got out of my landrover, and shouted and waved my arms, the lions would have run off, for almost all wild lions are still afraid of humans on foot; but my doing that would have made them more nervous and difficult to observe later on, and might also have meant that some of the more timid ones would have deserted and lost their hard-caught kills. Therefore I usually tried instead to edge the car in between the lions and their kill so that I could get out on the blind side and examine the carcass, unseen by the undisturbed lions. Sometimes this was impossible, either because of the terrain, or because the lion refused to be separated from its kill, or because it carried the carcass away to cover. In these cases I saw what I could through binoculars and returned the next day to try to collect further information from any fragments which remained.

The first thing to establish was what actually killed the victim, for lions will scavenge food from any carcass they can find, as well as appropriating kills from other smaller predators. Vulture droppings on or around the carcass, or the eye removed, suggested natural causes and that vultures had found the carcass first. Handfuls of plucked-out hair on the ground indicated a leopard's kill. Hyaenas carry away pieces of a prey animal while lions do not, so missing limbs suggested that hyaenas had been at the kill. Pieces of fresh grass in the mouth of the victim indicated a sudden death; tracks in soft ground could sometimes show whether there was a struggle and with what predator. Claw marks and tooth wounds on the victim also indicated the cause of death. Lions kill their prey by biting and holding the throat or nose, and on looking inside the skin I could often see the haemorrhaged marks of their canine teeth. Nonetheless, despite such clues as these, there were some carcasses whose cause of death I could not discover.

I established the species and sex of the prey animal, estimated its age approximately from the amount of wear on its teeth, and obtained a rough idea of its condition from the amount of fat stored in the bone marrow of its limb bones. I also noted how much meat had been eaten from it and where. In addition, of course, I made routine observations on the lions present.

To determine what effects lion predation was having on the prey populations I carried out counts of all the larger mammal species in my area. Regular censuses from my vehicle as I drove along a standard route, and less frequent aerial counts from a light aircraft, gave me an indication of how many prey animals were potentially available as lion food, and thus I could work out roughly what proportion of them were actually killed by lions. Later in this book I describe lions' hunting methods and their effects on their prey species; first, however, I must describe how they spend the much greater part of their lives when not hunting or feeding.

3 · Life in the pride

A unique feature of lions, compared with all other kinds of cats, is that they are social – they are usually to be found in groups which may contain females, cubs, adult males, or any combination of all three. The largest number of lions I ever saw all together at one time was thirty-six, but this was most exceptional, and anywhere between two and twelve is much more usual. The animals in a group normally all belong to the same 'pride', a kind of permanent extended family. The Oxford English Dictionary defines pride as 'a "company" of lions in the wild state'; without disagreeing with this definition, George Schaller and I have somewhat modified it to refer to a *lasting* social grouping of lions, not a temporary group of them, and in this book the term 'pride' is always used to indicate a permanent social unit, like a human family, not to refer to any group of lions (like a 'flock' of birds). The members of both lion prides and human families are not all together at any one time, but they all belong nevertheless.

PRIDES

The nucleus of a pride consists of a number of related adult females – related because they were born and reared in that same pride, which has probably lasted for generations. Of course, there have not yet been scientists observing lions for as long as that – our records in the Serengeti cover only about twelve years, a couple of lion generations – but during that time the various lion prides we observed have remained in existence, and in particular we did not find any cases of strange unrelated females joining a pride. At one point during my study, two lionesses who had lived together as a group separate from the next-door pride did join it as full members. Fortunately, though, I knew the past history of these two lionesses, and was aware that they were the offspring of that pride and had been driven from it but not from its area three years earlier; they were not really strangers to it. Associated with the group of related breeding females there are also their cubs growing up, some of which will in their turn eventually take the place of their mothers, aunts or grandmothers as the core of the pride.

Attached to the pride, too, are a number of mature breeding adult males. These males are *not* related to the lionesses, having grown up in a different pride, as I outline in Chapter 4, but they are related to one another and grew up together. For reasons I go on to describe, the males are members of the pride for only a few years – not permanently like the females – but while there they are full members, and play a large part in defending the pride's range and excluding other lions from it.

Lion prides are flexible in their structure. In the Serengeti, a 'typical' pride would consist of seven adult females, two adult males and a very variable number of cubs. But typical prides, like typical people, are comparatively rare things. The largest pride I knew contained a dozen females, while the smallest had only two. The number of males varied much less, most prides having two or three. I knew only one pride which had a single adult male with it for a long period. Two prides each had six males, but I have never heard of prides with more than that number. Thus, including cubs, a pride could contain up to forty-five animals in all, though this was most unusual even in the Serengeti and, to judge from others' reports, exceedingly rare anywhere else.

It will be obvious that the size of the whole pride must fluctuate with time, as cubs are born or die, and as females and males die or leave. Synchronized births by some of the lionesses in a pride can double that pride's total numbers in the course of a month. Nonetheless, the number of adult females in a pride stays roughly constant from year to year.

Small prides may be fairly cohesive, but it is unusual to find all the lions in a large pride together at one time. Instead, I would come across smaller numbers of pride members in temporary groups, or singly somewhere within their pride area. It was only by being able to recognize individual lions, and by observing them over a period of time, that I could determine how large their prides really were. In some cases it took many months before I came across, for example, lioness A with

19 At dusk two lionesses stride purposefully in step

lioness B and so could be certain that they belonged to the same pride, although I would probably have guessed it already if both animals were using the same range.

The composition of temporary groups of lions, usually of between two and ten animals, is not a random matter but varies with the different individuals concerned. Some lions are more solitary than others. Some combinations of two or more lions together occur much more often than others, since lions form particular companionships or attachments with other individuals. Some pairs of lionesses were together almost every time I saw them. In addition, females are likely to be with their cubs, of course, and the more so the younger those cubs are; and two or more females each with cubs of the same age tend to be together often. Subadults usually go around in a group together, and adult males often do so too. But all the lions in a pride, whether in close companionship or not, meet one another often as they move around in their territory, and thus they form temporary groupings of widely differing compositions. When pride members meet one another, they interact peacefully, greeting, grooming or playing with one another as I describe later in this chapter. Certainly, by sight and by smell, they can recognize other pride members individually, and probably much more efficiently, than I could. They behave in a completely different, hostile way towards strange lions.

In many respects the adult males are less well integrated into the pride than are the females. For example, a male does not form companionships with particular lionesses in his pride, and indeed he is much more likely to be found in the company of another male. Even when male lions are at the same place as a group of females, they tend to be somewhat separated. While the lionesses may well be within a yard or two of one another and often touching, the male or males are more likely to be some dozens of yards off. Males often greet one another but rarely greet females, although they themselves are often greeted by those females. Similarly, they are only occasionally involved in mutual grooming or playing with cubs. Males do not take the lead in hunting or in group movements, but tend to lag behind and follow along after the females.

To some extent, then, a lion pride may be said to be composed of two fairly distinct 'subprides' – the females with all their young and the adult males. Lions are most amicable towards lions in the same 'subpride' as themselves although they are in no way hostile to those in the other. The males seem to associate with the females mainly in order to obtain food and to get access to any female who may be in oestrus. The greater companionship among males and among females than between those males and females is understandable in view of the past histories of those animals. The males are often close relatives who have been together since cubhood. So are the females. But the males are not related to the females and are comparative strangers to the pride. They gradually become more familiar with time, and I found that the longer the males remained with the pride, the more likely they were to be found with the lionesses.

INACTIVITY PATTERNS

Lions spend most of their lives inactive. On average, adults are on their feet for only about four hours a day, perhaps one hour of which they

48

20 A group of lions (eight of them in the picture) rests in the midday shade. Lions were not easy to find among thick vegetation and deceptive logs

spend feeding. The rest of the time they are either resting or asleep. Cubs are much more active than adults, and spend a considerable amount of time playing. Tourists and others who see lions typically doing nothing are apt to castigate them as 'lazy'. I think it is more sensible to regard them instead as highly efficient animals which can meet all their needs in a few hours each day. It is difficult to see what else lions should spend their time doing once they have satisfied their hunger.

An added reason for the assertion that lions are lazy animals is that people tend to be looking at them at the wrong time of day. We might well label the human species as a very dull inactive one if we were to study humans only between midnight and dawn – the period which for us corresponds to the lions' daytime resting period. Most movement by lions takes place at night, particularly in the three hours after dusk and the five hours before and around dawn.

An adult male may cover a great distance in a night as he traverses his territory, on the lookout (or smellout?) for intruders, for oestrous females or for a kill made by some of the other members of his pride. On

49

the other hand, lionesses with their cubs do not generally move around in this apparently determined way. Almost all their travelling, I think, is to look for food, to go to a drinking place, or to retire to a patch of shade in which to spend the day. When, which way, and how far they go while hunting is variable and unpredictable, and this was one of my main problems. Lions usually start to move off at about dusk, as both the light and the temperature drop sharply: it was noticeable that when rain in the afternoon lowered the temperature the lions would often set off much earlier, well before dusk. Prior to this they would have been alert, perhaps watching or listening for potential prey animals, and after a while they set off in the appropriate direction towards them. A lion group travelling may maintain a steady walking speed of about two miles per hour, but more often they keep stopping and starting, sitting and listening, meandering and playing. The average distance they cover in a night is around three miles; they go further when they are hungrier, and of course stop travelling in order to feed if they manage to catch a victim. If they do, they usually spend a few hours eating that night and then travel little during the next night or two while their bellies are still full.

When daylight comes – quickly and often with a superbly coloured dawn – it finds the lions out in the open, and so did I if I was lucky. They are still fairly active at this time of day, and if they have one they chew at the remains of their night's kill, and play with one another, their breath visible as puffs of steam in the cool early morning air.

Being active, one of the things they may do at this time of day is drink. Sources of water are abundant in the wet season: there are streams, puddles and rock pools, and lions drink from them quite often in the course of their travels. In the dry season, water is less easily accessible but still obtainable from stagnant pools in the beds of the larger rivers or from springs. In some regions lions can go for several days without water, but this was unnecessary in the Serengeti. I think the lions I observed drank every day, if not more often, as they moved around their area. Drinking is by lapping as in domestic cats, and therefore a slow process; nonetheless there were many occasions on which lions could drink without my being able to detect their doing so.

Another topic I shall deal with here for want of a better place is grass-eating. Many times I have seen lions 'grazing', biting off and eating quite large grass leaves. They must get virtually nothing which is nutritively valuable from it, for I examined the grass when it reappeared in their droppings and it was scarcely chewed or altered in any way. They eat grass especially when full, and the faeces it reappears in are particularly the dark smelly liquid ones which follow soon after a large meat meal. I do not know what purposes if any grass serves inside a lion.

In the early part of the morning, the lions bask in the low sunlight, apparently warming themselves. A couple of hours later the sun and the air are hotter, and the lions retreat into the shade. Thinking ahead does not seem to be their strong point, and by the time they actually brace themselves to move it is obviously uncomfortable to do so. Watching a lion decide whether or not to shift into the shade, I could almost feel the conflict going on in his mind. He (or she) would clearly be too hot where he was, and apparently uncomfortable; flies might well be pestering him, and sometimes a full stomach would also help to anchor him. For several minutes the lion would look at a distant inviting patch of shade, look away, shake his head and ears, and try a different posture for a while. I knew that he would eventually plod heavily through the heat to the shade, and I was often amazed that the lion did not do so earlier in the day, before the higher temperature made the short journey such an obviously greater effort.

Lions in the Serengeti did not have fixed daytime resting places: instead they would spend the daylight hours in any suitable patch of shade near to where dawn had stranded them. Usually this would be under one of the larger *Acacia* trees near a drainage line, but sometimes it would be in a thicket or down in an overgrown, sunken and partially dry stream. In very hot, still weather, damp sandbanks in river beds were particularly favoured. This would be infuriating for me, because I could not observe lions in thick vegetation; it was also much more difficult to find them at all, because I would get very poor range from a radio-collar which was lying with its wearer down in a sunken river course. As if to compensate, there were of course the times when a radio-collared lion was high up on a kopje or occasionally up a tree, so enabling me to detect and track it from miles away.

In some areas, such as in Lake Manyara National Park in Tanzania, and in Queen Elizabeth (now Ruwenzori) National Park in Uganda, the lions spend many of their days resting up in trees, like cumbersome overweight leopards. This seems to be a learned local tradition. If a lion can manage to find it comfortable, there are several advantages to sleeping in a tree. First of all, it is cooler higher up because there is more breeze, especially if there is a large amount of vegetation at ground level. Second, there are not so many flies to bother the sleeper; why this

21 A lioness sleeps in leopard-like manner on a branch, gaining a cool breeze and respite from flies

22 A lioness lies in the On Back posture, which shows the white heat-reflecting stomach fur

should be I do not know, but I noted a number of times that a lioness up a tree had fewer flies on her than did her companion on the ground below. In addition, a lion up a tree has no need to be alert for or take evasive action against animals such as buffaloes, or perhaps even minibuses in tourist areas. The only disadvantage to spending the day in a tree is that most lions transparently find it uncomfortable, especially when their stomachs are full. In the Serengeti I knew only two young lionesses who were habitually lodged over a branch when I found them, and even they grew out of the practice. Probably in my area there were too few suitable large trees with branches broad enough for lions to learn to rest on them in real comfort; certainly the practice is rare there.

Lions have a number of different resting postures, and the terms 'sitting' or 'lying' proved to be inadequate and sometimes confusing for my purposes. The lion's commonest sleeping position is flat on its side, with its flank, head and all four legs resting limply on the ground. This I called the 'Head On Side' posture. A fully immobilized lion looks much like this, and so does a dead one; there are stories, partly mythical I fear, of people in the Serengeti getting out of their cars to examine a 'dead' lion, whereupon the corpse raised its head and ran off in as much haste, surprise and fear as the people did. A lion who is sleepy and very hot often lies on its back with one to all of its legs either sticking loosely up in the air or resting against a tree trunk. In this 'On Back' posture the surprisingly white but sparse fur around the lion's belly and groin is exposed and presumably allows more of the lion's excessive heat to be radiated away. A hot lion with a very bloated stomach often seems to find this position uncomfortable, and panting hard it will adopt either a 'Sphinxed' or a squatting posture which takes some of the weight off its belly. A sleeping lion who is cool lies with both its hind legs drawn in close together on the same side of its body, with its forelegs both underneath the slumped shoulders and neck, and with the cheeks or chin resting on the paws ('Head On Paws'). Cubs will sometimes huddle together on top of one another during a cold night or when it is raining. (Lions in the Serengeti appeared to dislike rain but they did not try to seek shelter from it. They would usually have had to travel quite a long way to find an effective sheltering place, in a cave or under a rock overhang.)

The standard resting posture of a more awake lion was what I called 'TLFS' – 'Tail-end Lying Front Sphinxed'. Both hind legs lie on one side of the body, but the front end rests symmetrically on the brisket and on

53

the elbows and forearms, one on each side of the chest. The lion may hold its head up and look around alertly, or it may sit thus with its eyes closed and head drooping, or anything in between. If a lion in this posture becomes more alert, perhaps because it has seen potential prey, it can change quickly into the 'Sphinxed' position by swivelling the rear end of its body smoothly over its drawn-in hind legs; thus it can be completely ready either to crouch low so as to avoid being seen, to squat so as to be able to see over an obstruction, or to start running if necessary.

As the late afternoon becomes cooler, the lions start to become less inactive and more interesting – watching motionless lion stomachs for hour after hour is not an exciting occupation. Head On Side and On Back give way to TLFS. The lions yawn occasionally, stretching open their mouths to an extraordinary extent and revealing their entire oral armoury. They sometimes sneeze, which on occasion was the first indication I had that there were lions nearby, invisible in the long grass. They stand and stretch luxuriantly in their huge feline manner, in either or both of two ways. In one, the lion stands with all four feet close together, the head points downwards, and the back arches sharply and stiffly upwards. In the second way, the rump is forced high and back-wards, the shoulders sink low and the forelegs are stretched out for-wards along the ground; the claws are extended and scrape into the soil. A rather similar form of stretching is the tree-clawing which lions frequently perform on vertical tree trunks, raking their claws down-wards through the bark or wood like a cat against a table leg. I do not know what they do it for. Perhaps it leaves a scent mark from the glands on the paws, as a kind of olfactory signpost to other lions. Possibly it also sharpens the claws. Certainly it is an activity which is highly contagious, and other lions frequently join one which is tree-clawing and start to do the same themselves. By now they have begun to interact with other members of their group, the topic of the next section.

SOCIAL INTERACTION

Lions are intensely as well as uniquely social, and show every sign of enjoying one another's company. Not only do the members of a group stay together but they stay close together, sometimes even uncomfortably close, and interact often and amicably. When two lions meet or pass, they greet one another by rubbing heads together. Each inclines its head towards the other and one rubs the cheeks or the side of its face above the eye against the head of the second animal. The behaviour looks both affectionate and sensual, especially when the greeting becomes a prolonged and elaborate rubbing together of the necks and sometimes the whole sides of the bodies of the participants. Sometimes the greeting is almost symbolic; a lion passing a resting companion may do little more than lower the near side of its head and lightly brush past the recipient. The latter often seems to expect or at least to anticipate a greeting, raising or tipping its head appropriately in advance. Small cubs often cannot reach the face of an adult, and then they head-rub against its legs or under its chin instead. Cubs more than adults tend to use their whole bodies in head-rubbing, which in this way is very similar to a domestic cat's rubbing against the legs of humans or tables. Unlike domestic cats, though, I never saw lions rub against inanimate objects in their environment.

When a lion rejoins a group from which it has been absent for some time there may be a great orgy of head-rubbing, lasting for several minutes, as the newcomer goes to each companion in turn and thoroughly greets him or her. Oestrous females soliciting mating from males, or cubs soliciting food from adults, use similar, very prolonged head- and body-rubbing to convey their needs and to try to persuade

23 A lioness approaches another resting in the grass and rubs heads in greeting. Note the tattered and therefore easily recognizable ear of the recipient

the other animal to respond to them. Thus cubs greet an adult, and especially their mother, more often than she reciprocates, and likewise an adult male tends to let the females come and greet him rather than initiating the greeting himself, although he does head-rub often with his male companions.

When one lion rubs heads with another it demonstrates its peaceful intentions, in much the same way as shaking hands among humans does. Perhaps rubbing noses together, in Eskimo fashion, would be a better analogy, being more tactually pleasing (I imagine, to Eskimos, who have more appropriately shaped noses). In either case, the gesture probably helps to maintain social cohesion in the group. In lions it may do this in a largely biochemical way. Parts of the skin of the face, especially above the eyes, produce secretions; rubbing heads together is likely to transfer some of these secretions from one lion to another. If these secretions have a scent which lions can detect, head-rubbing could help to ensure that all pride members share a characteristic pride odour, which may be important in distinguishing between pride members and strangers. Thus head-rubbing might be a process of exchanging a kind of perfumed password.

Greeting is often followed by grooming. One animal licks the head and neck of the second, which may then reciprocate with the result that the grooming becomes mutual. Lions have strong rough tongues (as I felt many times when an immobilized animal licked its lips and my fingers while I was measuring its teeth). Licking with such a tongue must comb as well as clean the fur, and its effects are clearly seen after a kill. While feeding at a carcass, a lion often gets its face thoroughly red-stained with blood, but a spell of social grooming soon removes this. Lions do little washing of their own faces with their paws like domestic cats, perhaps partly because they are less good at squatting; their forepaws are usually resting on the ground with little freedom of movement. A lion trying to groom its own face is really only wiping its face against its paws, rather than vice versa. Grooming of the head and upper neck, the only parts of its body which a lion cannot reach directly with its own tongue, is much more efficiently and more often done by its social companions.

As a critical biologist watching them, I often felt that this mutual cleaning was somewhat unnecessary in that the animals were clean already. Almost certainly grooming has other social functions as well, such as helping to keep all the lions in a pride thoroughly familiar with and amicable towards one another. This is important because survival

24 A lioness grooms her own face by licking her paw and then rubbing her face along it

25 One lioness grooms the neck of a second, who shows every sign of enjoying the treatment

26 A young adult male grooms his shoulders and what he can reach of the front edge of his mane

and breeding success for lions depends on their co-operation with one another in all sorts of ways that I shall describe. Lions probably also find it pleasing to be groomed – the closed eyes and languorously stretched neck of the recipient certainly suggest so – and the head and neck where almost all social grooming takes place in lions are the parts of the body where my own domestic cat prefers to be stroked.

Social grooming takes place most among females and large cubs.

Small cubs get groomed a lot by females, but do little grooming in return. Adult males rarely groom others or get groomed in return, as the odd dirty tangles in their mane witness; it may be less pleasant to both the groomer and the groomed to lick all that long coarse hair around the neck. Lions do not often groom other parts of their companions' bodies, with the exception that females groom their small cubs all over. Grown animals keep their own bodies clean, beautifully so in healthy lions. As well as removing dirt, grooming gets rid of almost all parasites such as ticks before they can affix themselves, and the number of ticks I could find on an immobilized lion was usually minute.

Another social activity is playing. The young of a great many species are playful, but it seems that as adults the social carnivores, and humans, are more inclined to play than most other animals. However, in lions, adult females play a great deal more than males do, unlike in wolves, wild dogs and humans, where they play less. Adult male lions almost never play; they very occasionally poke at a cub with a paw, and sometimes do something which I called PLOTO, 'Provocative Lying On Top Of' another male, who usually squirms out from underneath but does not otherwise respond. Lionesses, on the other hand, play frequently, especially at dusk and dawn. One female ambushes or stalks towards another, then rushes and chases it, both flitting through the half-light in a remarkably light-footed manner. Females play with cubs too, particularly by poking or dabbing with a paw at the cub, who swats back defensively, often lying on its back with its feet in the air. Cubs ambush and chase lionesses and other cubs, swat at one another, and lie grappling, cuffing and wrestling in twos or threes. Their play has much the same disorganized and erratic character as domestic kittens' romping; and as in kittens, younger cubs, being less mobile than older ones, do relatively more grappling and less chasing of one another.

Companions are the most usual and probably the best things to play with, but cubs will play alone too. They often chew at and carry about sticks, and sometimes try to do the same with the tuft at the tip of an adult's tail. The sight of one cub carrying or playing with a stick often makes another cub chase it and try to take over and play with the object itself. One quite large and well-fed cub I watched completely thwarted an adult lioness which was trying to drag a heavy wildebeest carcass into the shade. Again and again, as soon as she managed to start the carcass moving, the cub leaped upon it and lay biting and wrestling with it, making her load so heavy and inconvenient to drag that eventually she abandoned it to the vultures. Not once did she make any attempt to deter the cub from hindering her, and probably she did not realize that it was making her task more difficult. Cubs who are no longer hungry often play with carcasses, or with detached bits of them, such as limbs, skull, tail or large pieces of skin. During the rare times of prolonged food shortage in the Serengeti, cubs in poor condition scarcely played at all, either with one another or with inanimate objects. No one knows why lions (or indeed any animals) play, but we can guess that it gives them practice at doing things such as hunting and fighting which will be useful to them in later life. Certainly many of the postures cubs use in play are similar to those used in later years when the lion is in earnest. The principles of using cover while stalking probably have to be learnt and are likely to be similar whether the unwitting animal being approached is another lion cub or an alert prey animal.

SIGNALS

For almost any group of animals to co-ordinate their behaviour, there must be a flow of information back and forth among the various members of the group. In lions, as in humans, some of this communication is by means of precise signals, but much other general information can be obtained merely by observing other individuals. For example, I may receive the information that someone is hungry either by hearing him give a precise verbal signal to that effect (i.e. saying 'I am hungry'), or by observing him as he licks his lips, watches my every mouthful or makes frantic gestures at waiters. In the second case he is not deliberately signalling to me, yet I have gathered information about him; whether and how I use it is, of course, a different matter.

A lion's posture provides a continuous, if sometimes stagnant, stream of information. The usual relaxed resting posture of a lion 'in neutral' has the head pointing somewhat downwards, the ears at a medium angle and flicking occasionally to keep out flies, and the mouth either loosely closed or with the lower jaw drooping. When I see a lion in this posture I, and probably his companions too, know that he is unafraid and unaware of anything of interest around him, and that he is unlikely to move in the near future.

If such a lion sees or hears a possible prey animal or something else interesting, he (or more likely, she) rapidly becomes alert. She raises her nose, bring her ears forward, and an indefinable look of intentness takes over her face, while the limp relaxed appearance of her body is

27 Three cubs play with a lioness who dabs at one of them with her paw

28 A cub pounces on and plays with a wildebeest carcass, thereby frustrating the lioness's attempts to drag it to cover

replaced by a more taut, alert one. Other lions pay attention to these changes. Although it sometimes seems to be almost like telepathy, I presume that it must in fact be by detecting the alteration in her expression and body tone that her companions are alerted to the possibility of action.

If a lion is walking, its posture and gait also convey information to me or to other lions watching. Sometimes it is rambling along in an erratic meandering manner, and sometimes heading determinedly towards a particular place. It may be walking with the unhurried, upright, head-high gait of a pride male who is publicizing rather than hiding his presence, or hurrying nervously through other lions' territory. Similarly, a stealthy posture with head low differs according to whether the lion is stalking towards prey, approaching an intruder, or taking evasive action from a dangerous adversary.

Faces can convey more precise information, and facial signals are often directed at particular individuals. Lions are one of the easiest animals in which to observe a wide variety of facial expressions; this is partly because they have large and highly expressive faces, and partly because, being social animals, they use these expressions frequently when they interact with one another. The most noticeable expressions tend to be the antagonistic ones, as a lion uses threats in order to get its own way yet at the same time, if possible, to avoid physical conflict. Defensive threat expressions can be seen most often at food, if a lion who is feeding at a piece of a kill is approached by another. It holds its ears firmly back against the sides of its head, which must help to keep them out of harm's way if a fight should develop. It opens its mouth and draws back its lips, which makes its main weapons clearly visible to its adversary; this also makes its nose wrinkled and its eyes narrowed. At the same time the lion produces a snarl or a hiss which reinforces its message, instantly clear to me as it obviously was to other lions, that further approach might well provoke violence. This full threat expression I have described is by no means a standard one which is switched on and off to order; rather, it varies depending on how aggressive, or fearful, or hungry the lion is, who its opponent is, and what the latter is doing. Often a lion makes only the vestige of this expression; for example, when discouraging a cub from making contact, it may merely retract the lips slightly on the side nearest the cub. It does not follow that, because a lion makes a defensive threat expression it will necessarily attack, even if the 'offender' persists, as it well may. As in humans too, a threat only means that violence is being considered, and the lion

62

may have second thoughts about the likely outcome of a fight with a much stronger animal. In a sense, many threats are a combination of warning and bluff.

There is less element of bluff in an aggressive threat. A lion who is about to attack another has a rather rigid posture, usually with the head held low, the ears back, the lips normal and the eyes wide open. Growls accompany and accentuate the threat. A much milder form of aggressive threat is a fixed stare which may be the reason why lions, like humans and other animals, often appear disturbed if people stare fixedly at their eyes.

I do not think tail movements are particularly important as signals. Lions use their tails as fly whisks, and apparently to help them balance when running fast, both of which are obvious non-signalling functions. A lion stalking prey may twitch the end of its tail as a domestic cat does, but no other lion seems to pay attention to it, and the prey is clearly not meant to do so either. Similarly, tail-lashing during a fight probably does not communicate much useful extra information, and nor I imagine does the high tail-waving of a female soliciting copulation. Sometimes, for example when lions are greeting and sniffing at one another, the tail may be jerked up over the back in a very conspicuous manner, for reasons which I do not understand.

I have referred to the snarls, hisses and growls which lions make when threatening or squabbling with one another. In addition there are other vocal signals. A cub makes a sharp miaowing if it is separated from its mother and does not want to be; usually one hears this noise when they are following along behind her, and even more often if the cub is lost and without companions. When cubs want to suckle, or are hungry and apparently trying to stimulate adults to catch food, the miaows are longer and more whining, grading into surprisingly deep-voiced snarls as the cubs struggle with one another for a food source such as a mother's nipple or a nibble at a carcass.

Adult lions are fairly vocal animals, too. They make very soft humming or puffing noises when they are in close contact with other group members, but I do not know what purpose these sounds serve. *Unlike* domestic cats, for a change, lions do not purr; the nearest thing to it, but occurring in a completely different context, is the steady rumbling noise made by a lioness on heat before and during mating. Other functionless noises, which as a lionwatcher I often heard my subjects make, are a regular throaty panting sound when a lion is very hot, occasional sneezes, and sometimes a short sigh as a lion lies down.

29 Pained at their struggling, a lioness snarls her protest at the five cubs trying to suckle from her. Note the expression with ears back, nose wrinkled and teeth bared; also her missing upper incisor tooth

By far the loudest signal, and the most characteristic noise lions make, is the roar. It is a powerful and inspiring sound, not a bit like the brief snarl with which the MGM lion introduces that company's films. The entire roar lasts for thirty or forty seconds, and is audible from a couple of miles away, and sometimes more. Usually lions are standing when they roar, but they can roar when sphinxed or TLFS, as they often are when they hear and respond to the roars of another group. Sometimes when the lion is sphinxed, one can see the effort of producing the sound rocking the body back and forth, in synchrony with the bursts of condensation as lungfuls of hot breath meet the cold air outside.

All adult lions can roar, males producing a somewhat deeper and louder sound. I could recognize some individuals from the quality of their roar, I thought, but it was difficult to test whether I was right or wrong. Almost certainly lions can also recognize the roars of their companions, and probably much better than I could. I carried out some experiments with a tape-recorder to try to prove that they could distinguish between the roars of pride members and those of strangers, but what I think these experiments really showed was that lions are quite good at distinguishing between real lions and tape-recorders, and at ignoring the latter!

I did not often hear lions roaring during the daytime; when they did it was usually following a squabble of some sort. Most roaring takes place at the times when lions are most active – after dusk, around dawn, and at odd intervals during the night. A pride roars up to a dozen times during a night, more if the pride is split up and the members apparently want to rejoin one another. But often their roaring seemed to me almost like group singing, in being both functionless and melodious.

Cubs cannot (or at least they don't) make proper roars until they are well over two years old, but they sometimes add their own noises to the chorus while their elders are roaring. It would probably be through such choruses that lions would learn to distinguish the different roars of different individuals in their pride, as I failed to demonstrate that they can do. A lioness looking for her cubs or encouraging her cubs to follow her sometimes makes much softer roars, or merely loud moans, as she walks along; I do not think I ever heard a male making these soft roars.

A further kind of signalling which lions make use of is by means of scent marks, and this I describe in Chapter 5.

COMPETITION

Other than at kills, I saw remarkably little competition between lions belonging to the same pride. The adult lionesses in a pride are all equals, despite the wide range in their ages, from three to fifteen or so. In many other species of animals – in chickens, for example – there is a 'pecking order': one dominant bird has priority over all the others and can displace any bird from a perch or food source. The second top bird can, and does, behave in the same way towards all others except its superior; and similarly down a whole hierarchy to the unfortunate bird at the bottom of the pecking order who can be pecked by all and can lord it over nobody. Similarly, within most stable animal groups, the individuals learn by competing who can dominate whom, and remember this when they meet next time. The terms 'top dog', 'cock of the roost', 'master stag', 'king crow', 'underdog', 'whipping boy' and, misleadingly, 'scapegoat' suggest something of the wide range of species in which dominance hierarchies occur. Lions, however, are unusual in that they do not have any kind of hierarchy like this, or at least none that I have been able to detect. No particular lioness, for example, regularly displaces any other at kills or at resting places; all of them reproduce; and any of them may take the lead when hunting or travelling. This does not necessarily mean that all of them do everything quite equally – for example a sick animal may often lag behind, or may produce cubs much less often than her companions – but although some females may do much less well than the average, none does much better. I could not pick out a particular lioness in a pride whom I considered to be the leader or the chief of that pride, although I could point out a slow elderly one who would probably be last. On the whole the females are an almost communistic group of equals with equal rights, who depend on one another for more efficient hunting and for more successful reproduction, both of which I shall describe in later chapters. The lionesses in a pride are also a stable group of friendly relations, usually with little to compete over, so harmony is not surprising.

But, as in any community, when a commodity is in short supply, things become less peaceful. At kills there may be a little or a considerable amount of squabbling among animals who earlier were completely amicable towards one another. I found this competition at kills somewhat confusing at first, until a number of general trends or rules began to emerge. The first of these trends, and a rather obvious one, is that there is a great deal more competition among hungry animals than among better fed ones. A second is that there is much less competition over large kills than over small ones. If a lion pride which has been getting a reasonable food supply over the previous days or weeks kills a large prey animal such as a buffalo or a zebra, all the members of the pride usually feed on it at the same time. They may growl, snarl and swat at one another in the course of their feeding, causing noise and sometimes scratched noses and nicked ears, but little real injury. All get some food, which is the usual state of affairs for most lion prides at most times of the year.

The third rule is that first possession of an item of food makes its owner temporarily dominant over its equals. This applies when the kill or pieces of it are small and when the lions are not very hungry. I have often seen the value of prior possession when a carcass has been pulled apart, and when a lion is feeding at each piece of it. One animal, having finished its piece, approaches another who is still feeding; the second growls at the potential usurper or may lunge at it if it is very close. The approacher gives way, as though recognizing that ownership bestows extra strength or determination upon the owner of the food. Some kills are too big to be 'owned' by a single lion; the dividing line seems to be roughly whether the lion can carry or easily drag away the food item. Once it has done so, it apparently looks on that piece of food as its own. But when two or more lions first catch a small prey animal such as a gazelle, or when they find a carcass with some meat on it, a struggle to establish ownership often ensues. It is usually resolved when the disputed kill is torn into two or more pieces by lions pulling in opposite directions. This may take some time, though, because each contestant attempts to hold down the food, using mouth and paws and often half-covering it in the process. A great deal of growling and some swatting takes place, but I was surprised to see that lions did not make outright attacks with the teeth at the body of their rival. This is partly, no doubt, because it is disadvantageous to a lion to injure its companions badly; but also if a lion removes its weapons from the carcass to attack its rival, it is likely to find that the latter manages to run off with the carcass and so to achieve complete ownership. Two adult males I watched spent at least half an hour in one of these struggles for ownership of a small topi carcass which was almost hidden from view under their bodies; they heaved and struggled and rested alternately, their growling being accentuated whenever one of them made a move. Eventually the carcass came apart, and each got an unequal share of it.

This third rule I have just described applies among equals. The fourth rule is that larger lions are more equal than smaller ones. Even if a female, for example, has established ownership of a piece of food and can keep away her equals by threats, a male can often take it away from her. He simply grabs it or heaves it away from her, benefiting from his much greater size and strength. Once he has got it in his possession, his threats are enough to keep away the previous owner. There is little that the weaker animal can do in these circumstances, except to try to run off with all or part of the carcass; it would be foolish for a female to attack a male who was much stronger than herself, for she would probably get injured and still lose her food. The (male) 'lion's share' is what he can get, not what he is given.

Lionesses, though, may rob as well as be robbed. A female does not necessarily respect the claims to ownership of a cub which has got hold of a piece of a carcass, but may take it from the cub in the same manner as I have described above. The plundering system is based mainly on size, but also on hunger and on determination. Each lion in a pride presumably knows from past encounters something about the strength of every other animal, and can gauge roughly how likely it is to

67

retaliate. Temporary coalitions can make up for lack of individual strength: I have seen three lionesses drive a male off a carcass which he had appropriated from one of them.

Such a dynamic and self-interested food distribution system does not necessarily result in all lions receiving their appropriate shares. Cubs are always at a disadvantage, both because they arrive at kills after the lionesses and because they are obviously smaller and weaker than all the adults, who rob them of the little they can get. When the kills are large this does not matter, because the cubs get their food supply, although perhaps later than the adults. But when the kills are scarce and small – if the lions are feeding on gazelles, for example – the cubs may not get any food from them at all, and if these extreme conditions continue for a long time the cubs may die of starvation. They stop playing as they get leaner, and their skinny, scrawny, and often inert bodies present a pathetic picture. Lack of vitamins, probably, combined with mange parasites can make them lose almost all their hair, and so also lose more body heat, which without food they can ill afford. Internal parasites multiply, and the skin-covered walking skeletons get weaker and so arrive at kills later still. Meanwhile the adults, although thin, are in relatively good condition, and so their hunting ability is unlikely to be impaired; it would not benefit the cubs to receive more food from each kill if it meant that feebler lionesses could make fewer

30 A two-year-old cub dying of starvation, unable to get enough food from the small kills made by the lionesses in its pride

kills. The starvation of the cubs is caused partly by the social organization of lions, which is not well adapted to dealing with long periods when kills are small and few and far between; but in most lion habitats such conditions rarely occur. Cubs are tough and resilient little creatures which do not die at all easily and I was amazed at how quickly, once large prey animals became available again, they recovered their fur, their playfulness and their health.

In one important respect, adult male lions often belie their self-centred image in a somewhat surprising way. A male who has taken possession of a carcass and ferociously prevented lionesses from feeding at it will often, nonetheless, permit access to it by small cubs. He may threaten a cub who approaches, whereupon the cub stops and at once rolls over onto its back in submissive posture, only to resume worming its way forward again when the male relaxes. Males seem to be more tolerant than females towards cubs feeding from food which is in their possession. In this way an adult male sometimes enables the cubs to consume food which they would otherwise be unable to get; on the other hand, of course, if the male had not been there at all, there might have been more left for the cubs after the females had finished feeding. I am not sure whether or not males are a 'good thing' from the point of view of lionesses and cubs, but certainly they are an inescapable component in lions' social organization and reproduction, as I outline in the next two chapters.

Although I have described lions' competition over food at some length, I hope I have not given a misleading impression of lion society, which I would stress is usually peaceful within a pride. This peace is rippled by squabbles at kills, turbulent ones in extreme circumstances. The rest of lions' lives, however, the vast majority of minutes in the ten to fifteen years of their existence, are spent in harmony with their companions, usually in a state of placid inactivity. But this would be a tedious book if I were to write at great length about lions peacefully doing nothing together!

4 · The life cycle

Breeding in lions is intimately linked with their social organization. The word 'cycle' in the title is almost misleading for it suggests a tidy repeating sequence of events, of matings followed by gestation, of the birth and then rearing of cubs, and the maturing of adults which in turn reproduce and complete the cycle. While in a sense this must happen if the species does not die out, life for lions as well as for other species is not really as simple as this. It bears some relation to the chaos of, say, a flower shop with flowers competing with one another to be sold. Many flowers never manage and are doomed, some early and others late, to oblivion. Some flowers are brilliant but only for a short time, while others are more sombre but last for longer, and potential purchasers, like natural selection, may favour one or the other of these depending on the situation in which they want to put the flowers. Chance may play a large part in the selection, but so will other factors. Some flowers have short stems and run out of water which is taken up by their longer stemmed neighbours, while others have stems so long that they break. Some flowers get overshadowed and overlooked behind others; some form coalitions by looking good together, so both they and their companions get selected. On certain days there are lots of indiscriminate buyers and on other days there are only a few choosy ones. The general cycle of flowers entering and leaving the flower shop continues smoothly, but the fate or future of each particular flower is influenced by all manner of different pressures. So it is with lions in the wild. Some leave many offspring, while some leave few or none, for a wide variety of reasons which I shall look at while describing events in the life cycle of lions.

70

It became quite easy for me to recognize a mating pair of lions, even when they were apparently doing nothing. The pair would be very close together, and they would probably be on their own – not, I think, because they seek seclusion but because they have got left behind in their preoccupation when the rest of the group moved on. They would often be out in the sun instead of in the shade, where I would expect most lions to be; maybe something happens to the lioness's temperature control mechanism when she is 'in oestrus' (or 'in heat' as it is

31 A male wrinkles his nose in a 'flehmen' expression after sniffing the urine of an oestrous female. Note the pieces of dirt entangled in his mane where he cannot groom himself

32 a,b,c,d A mating pair of lions. The male reclines in TLFS posture, while the female lies on her back. She rises and solicits the male, running quickly past his face, with tail raised, sometimes rubbing herself against him. He rises and follows quickly as she trots playfully away from him

33 a&b A copulating pair of lions. Note the biting movements by the male near the neck of the female. At ejaculation he yowls loudly and grimaces (showing his missing upper incisor tooth). The lioness snarls semi-aggressively at this stage, and would turn and swat at him if he did not dismount rapidly

appropriately called). I use the term 'in oestrus' to indicate any lioness who is in the behavioural, and presumably physiological, state of being prepared to mate with a male. He recognizes this state partly by her behaviour and partly, I think, by her smell. Wherever she moves he follows, not more than a few yards behind and often almost beside her.

If she urinates, he sniffs several times at the urine and then raises his head in a very striking manner which is termed 'flehmen', grimacing with his mouth open and his lips pulled back revealing all his teeth. His nose is wrinkled which makes his eyes appear partly closed. Any lion might make this flehmen response after sniffing at any new or powerful smell, but I saw it most frequently in the context I have just described. Other species of animal also make similar facial gestures in response to particular smells, and no one really knows why.

One of the pair may be much less inclined to mate than the other. When a female's oestrous period is just beginning, she often refuses to allow the male to copulate, although he follows her in a very persistent manner. On the other hand I have seen males who seemed fairly disinterested and who could only be induced to mate after prolonged soliciting by the lioness – greeting him repeatedly, rubbing against him with her head and flanks with her tail held out stiffly, and circling quickly round him when he is slow to respond. She then crouches in a sphinxed posture in front of him for a few seconds until he mounts or she resumes her soliciting again, making a steady rumbling sound throughout. While copulating, the male squats over the crouched female with his front legs straight and hind legs flexed. He usually achieves ejaculation within a few seconds, at which point he makes a sudden and distinctive yowling sound, which was a good indication that a lion whom I could not see was mating. He also makes biting movements at or near the female's neck, sometimes merely a gaping in the air and sometimes actually holding the lioness's neck skin in his teeth. The action seems to be a relic of the copulatory neck bite seen in domestic cats, where the tom holds the female's neck; this stops her from moving, in the same way that a kitten being carried dangling from its mother's mouth automatically, or rather by reflex, keeps quite still as long as there is a grip on the scruff of its neck.

The male lion dismounts quickly after copulation, and with good cause, because the female is liable to turn on him with a snarl or sometimes a swat. She then rolls over onto her side or her back, and the male after a short while reclines into the TLFS posture beside her. They relax like this for about ten to fifteen minutes on average, after which time they begin to become rather restless again. They sit up, look around and at each other, and then repeat the performance of the previous paragraph.

I was surprised to find that there would often be another male waiting nearby, between twenty and a hundred yards away, making no attempt to mate with the lioness in oestrus. The attendant male may be waiting for his companion to cease his sexual preoccupations and rejoin him as much as waiting for a chance to take his place. There seemed to be extraordinarily little competition between pride males for females in heat, considering the amount of fighting for matings which occurs in some species. (I discuss why in Chapters 9 and 10.) In one respect, an oestrous lioness is (unflatteringly) similar to a small piece of meat: the first male in possession of her is dominant over other males. They respect his prior possession and do not come too close; indeed they would be attacked if they did. Five or ten yards seems to be the dividing line. Sometimes an oestrous female, closely followed by her attendant male, walks towards another waiting male; the latter then has to move off quite quickly or he is liable to find himself attacked for being within what the male in possession obviously considers intolerably close proximity to 'his' lioness.

The lioness probably has more say in the matter of whom to mate with than I have implied. She may well be with a different partner on successive days, but the changes rarely occur more often than that. Sometimes the male appears to get bored, while on other occasions the female is responsible for the change. A couple of times, for example, I have seen a lioness get up quickly and trot over to a waiting male, apparently before her attendant consort realized what was happening. At once the tables were turned, and the new male was in possession and dominant over the previous boss. Presumably the lioness can also influence which male she first encounters when she is coming into oestrus. She does not seem to have a strong preference, though, and over a period of a few years every lioness I knew mated with more than one of the males in her pride. If an oestrous female comes across an outsider male – a nomadic animal, for example, or a male of a neighbouring pride – she will accept him quite readily instead. Similarly the pride males will mate with any oestrous female they meet, whether or not she belongs to their own pride, although they would drive off an intruding female not in heat. Overall, the males get a roughly equal share of matings. None does much better than his companions, although a lion who is slow or sick over a long period may do quite a bit worse.

Oestrous periods – the periods during which a lioness is prepared to mate – are very variable in length. Some last only a day or so, while others may last over a week. Most are between two and five days, during which time mating takes place on average every fifteen minutes, day and night. A simple calculation shows that a lioness mates at least 300 times during an average oestrous period, either all with the same male or with two or more different males. And yet, in spite of this very energetic mating performance, she is unlikely to produce young. Only about a fifth to a quarter of oestrous periods result in cubs being born, which means well over a thousand matings per litter of cubs – a strikingly inefficient process. I shall discuss in Chapter 9 the probable evolutionary causes of this inefficiency, because we would not expect natural selection to have allowed the reproductive performance of this big cat to have fallen so low, far below that of other animals, unless there were quite strong reasons. But it is worth mentioning here the more immediate possible causes of the lions' 'thousand-matings' phenomenon.

Lions, like all cats but unlike humans and many other mammals, are induced ovulators, that is to say, the release of an ovum or egg from the ovary of a lioness occurs only as a consequence of mating. A female who mates several times is more likely to ensure that this reflex mechanism operates properly to produce ovulation than a female who mates only once, so it is not surprising, I think, that reflex ovulators mate fairly often. But it *is* puzzling both that lions mate so much *more* often than other reflex ovulators, and that so many of their mating periods are unsuccessful. Naturally, I had no way of finding out in the wild whether or not a lioness whom I had seen mating had actually ovulated, nor whether or not she had conceived, nor whether she miscarried or aborted any unborn young. All are possible.

When a lioness comes into oestrus depends, of course, on what was the result of her previous oestrous period. If she became pregnant then, and produced cubs, her next oestrous period would not occur for a long time, until her cubs are almost reared. But if, as is more usual, she did not become pregnant, other things influence her. Lionesses in the wild, at least, do not appear to have regular oestrous cycles like most mammals; instead they are surprisingly irregular, coming into heat at intervals of anything from a couple of weeks to a few months. There is no such thing as a mating season: I could not point to a particular month of the year when I was more likely on average to encounter lionesses in oestrus. I got the impression that after the first rain following a long dry spell I tended to find mating lions unexpectedly often; but this may have been partly because they were more out in the open and visible then, and partly because rain brought more prey animals into the area. Better fed lions seemed to be mating more often than hungrier ones, which makes sense although I do not know what the mechanism for it might be.

Often when one lioness in a pride was in oestrus, one or more others would be as well, more often than would have occurred by chance. In other words, the oestrous periods of lionesses tended to be somewhat synchronized in this way with those of the other lionesses in the same pride. They would not be synchronized with the females in an adjacent pride, so their synchrony could not have been produced by large-scale climatic changes, nor by gross changes in prey numbers which tended to fluctuate similarly in neighbouring pride areas. There must, presumably, have been some within-pride factor operating. I can only guess at what this might have been, and there are three main possibilities. A female might well have responded to the smell of another female who was already in oestrus (a smell which is used in communication between animals and which produces some physiological or behavioural effect is called a pheromone). The second possibility is that the males produced a pheromone and that the females then responded to it synchronously. Or it is possible that some feature of their food supply – such as eating a pregnant buffalo, perhaps – tended to bring all the lionesses in a pride into a more similar physiological state. Whatever the cause, or causes, may have been, the result was that it surprisingly often happened that more than one female in a pride was in oestrus at a time: the pride males were then occupied with a female each and so were in no position to compete with one another over matings.

Lionesses, incidentally, are not the only species in which the group members tend to be in oestrus at the same time as one another; it happens with many animals, usually because they all respond in the same way and at the same time to some change in climate, food or day length. For example, each year in the Serengeti we witnessed the spectacle of most of the third of a million wildebeest cows mating during the month of May, probably triggered by the climate. However, in only a few species are the members of a social group known to be better synchronized with one another than with the members of their neighbouring groups, and most of these species are monkeys or apes. The best known to us are humans: it has been found that in at least some all-female institutions the women's menstrual periods gradually tend to become more synchronized, particularly with those of each woman's closest friend. In humans the causes of this synchrony are as little understood as they are in lions.

CUBS

A lioness or a tigress, although twice as large as an average woman, nonetheless produces her offspring in a far shorter time – only just over three-and-a-half months. This is a remarkably short gestation period for the size of the mother.

The figure for lions is based on records from zoos where it is possible to be certain of the dates on which lionesses did or did not mate; in the

34 A ten-week-old cub peers over the body of its reclining mother from whom it is suckling

Serengeti, of course, they often mated unobserved by me. I could not tell whether lionesses were carrying cubs until quite a late stage. Their pregnancy does not show until their mammary glands start to swell with milk, and for obvious reasons I could not handle or feel them. Their bodies do not swell very visibly with cubs; after all, a belly full of unborn cubs weighs considerably less than the forty pounds or so of meat which a lioness can and does fit into her stomach if the opportunity occurs. Nonetheless, from the lioness's point of view, pregnancy must be an extra burden, making it somewhat more difficult for her to sprint when hunting. This is probably one of the occasions when being a member of a social group is particularly valuable to her, for she can feed on prey animals which other members of her pride have captured or have helped her to capture.

There is no birth season, at least in the Serengeti, and probably not elsewhere either. Cubs may be born at any time of year, wet season or dry. Driving around the Serengeti I would come across cubs of the entire range of ages. However, within each pride the cubs tended to be in batches of similar age: for example, there might be several of perhaps a year and a half, a dozen of only a few months old, but few if any in between. Another synchrony effect: it seems that lionesses in a pride tend to produce cubs at very roughly the same time as their companions do. This is not a seasonal effect, because the cubs in an adjacent pride are unlikely to be born at that same time too. It is not a very precise synchronizing either: it is not that the cubs are all born within a few days of one another, but that they are likely to be produced within the same couple of months. The degree of 'clumping' of births varies. The most marked I came across was when eight out of ten lionesses in the Masai pride at Seronera produced a total of twenty-four cubs within a two-month period. Often, and particularly in smaller prides, I would find only that two females had given birth at the same time, after several months or more in which no cubs had been born in that pride.

What causes this rough birth synchrony by lionesses within the same pride? Obviously, to give birth at the same time, the females must have mated at about the same time as one another as well, and I have already referred to the fact that their oestrous periods tend to be synchronized. Mating at the same time would obviously tend to contribute towards producing simultaneous births, but it provides only part of the explanation. After all, most oestrous periods do not result in cubs, as I have said, and also the simultaneity of oestrous periods I observed was a short-term phenomenon over periods of only a few days. Therefore, since the gestation period cannot vary much, there must be some within-pride factor which either makes conception occur at approximately the same time or else tends to cause lionesses to abort if none of their companions is pregnant. I think it is likely that some sort of unconscious communication by pheromones takes place among the females, that in effect they 'tell' one another by means of smells whether they are pregnant or not and arrange their own reproduction accordingly. This, of course, is really only a guess as to what the immediate cause of their birth synchrony might be. But whatever the cause, it seems to be quite powerful, because when the clump of eight females in the Masai pride all gave birth at the same time, one of them was only just over three years old, and thus she still had several months to go before reaching the age at which most Serengeti lionesses produced their first litter.

A lioness can have between one and six cubs in a litter, with two to four being normal. She gives birth concealed in a thicket, or in thick vegetation in a kopje, and the cubs remain hidden for about the first six weeks of their lives. I did not go tramping about in thickets looking for

35 A six-week-old cub, newly brought to join the other lions in its pride, receives the attentions of an older cub trying to play with it, and of a lioness who sniffs at the unfamiliar-smelling stranger

new-born lion cubs, partly because I would have been very unlikely to find them, and partly because I would have been much more likely to have found myself uncomfortably facing an angry lioness or a disturbed buffalo. I rarely knew how many cubs there were in a litter until they were at least six weeks old, and by that time some might well have perished. A small number of entire litters did die before I ever saw them: I saw a lioness who had obviously given birth recently but I never afterwards came across her with cubs. In some cases, too, I knew that one or two cubs of a litter had disappeared before the survivors came out into the open. When the lioness was wearing a radio-collar I could sometimes pinpoint the exact place in, for example, an overgrown dry stream bed where she was lying with her cubs, and then I could see them well enough through the vegetation to count them. Another time at which it was sometimes possible to count new cubs was when a lioness was moving them, carrying the minute cubs one at a time. The cub dangles limply from her mouth, as she holds it by the whole of its

82

36 A lioness carries a three-week-old cub from one hiding place to another, grasping the cub's shoulders in her mouth. She is an easily recognizable female, lacking the black tuft at the tip of her tail, and having a large healed cut above her left nostril

shoulders, not just by the scruff of its neck as a domestic cat carries her relatively much larger kittens.

Lion cubs are completely helpless at birth, like the newborn young of almost all land-living carnivores. In a sense they are born much younger than are wildebeest calves, zebra foals, and young herbivores in general, which have to be mobile and able to escape from predators within a very few hours after birth. A lioness suckles her cubs at intervals, but spends quite a lot of her time apart from her newborn cubs but with other members of her pride. Every few days she transfers her young to a new hiding place, presumably to prevent each place acquiring a smell which might attract predators such as leopards or hyaenas which would kill any defenceless unguarded cubs they came across.

By the time they are about a month and a half old, the cubs can walk reasonably well, and their mother then leads them to join the rest of the pride. This will be the first time that the latter, or the attendant lion-watcher, has seen them. They are a lovely sight. Their fur is relatively longer and fluffier than that of adults, their feet look a little too large for their bodies, and the tail is short and tapering without the black tuft at the tip. All over the body there are traces of the spotted coat which presumably covered their ancestors very many generations back in their evolutionary history, and on the forehead these spots are quite clear, small and dark almost like those on the face of a young leopard.

A lioness is quite protective towards her small cubs if her companions go too close to them too quickly. I have seen her swat at an adult male whom her cubs approached, and I noticed that subadults were not tolerated close to them at first. The new cubs, on the other hand, do not appear to have any fear of other lions. They investigate them and try to play with them very soon. They are afraid of cars, though, and it takes a number of encounters with vehicles before they learn, I suppose from their mother's indifference as well as from their own experience, that these large, noisy, exhaust-producing animals are in fact harmless.

For many years there has been recounted the myth that another elderly lioness, termed an 'auntie', without cubs, assists one who is giving birth and helps her to rear her cubs. It is a myth with interesting smatterings of truth. No other lioness, it seems, does in fact attend the birth of the cubs, and I do not believe that there is anything she could very usefully do if she did. Nor, I think, does any other lioness visit the cubs in their hiding place before they are mobile. Once the cubs emerge, though, they join the pride as full members of it, and so may well be found in the company of a lioness who has not got cubs of her own. It is quite likely, too, that when the younger lionesses, including the cubs' mother, go off to hunt, the slower animals which remain behind will be the cubs and perhaps an elderly female, but she does not take any particular care of the cubs, beyond the care that all females and young in a pride bestow on their companions. On the other hand, the term 'auntie' is quite appropriate because any older lioness is quite likely to be another's aunt, or mother, or elder sister, or cousin, since all the females within a pride are related to one another. So if this purely imaginary helping lioness did exist, she probably *would* be some kind of aunt.

There is likely to be at least one other lioness who also has cubs of about the same age, because of the synchronizing of births I have described. When the cubs of the different mothers are mobile and have been brought out to join the pride, they tend to be reared communally. The cubs are then allowed to suckle from lionesses who are not their

84

37 A reclining lioness, with three cubs suckling from her, watches more cubs arriving to try to do the same. Lions are unusual in that the females allow others' cubs to suckle communally

38 A lioness tries ineffectively to deter cubs from suckling by rolling over, but her cubs climb over her in pursuit of her nipples

own mothers. Some females seem to be more tolerant than others in this respect. Lionesses are not neccessarily indiscriminate about which other cubs they allow to suckle from them: most are more tolerant of suckling by cubs which are of similar size or smaller than their own offspring than by larger cubs. On the other hand, and understandably I think, the cubs do not seem to be at all particular about where their milk supply comes from, and I have seen a cub going in turn from one prostrate brown milk-dispenser to another in search of a place where it could feed.

Communal suckling has a number of different effects. If some mothers produce more milk than others, it probably results in an averaging out of the amount of milk each cub receives. It also means that if a lioness dies, or if her milk flow ceases, her cubs do not necessarily perish, because they can suckle from her relations. For the lionologist, it means, annoyingly, that if he has not managed to recognize the cubs individually before they merge, it is almost impossible to tell later which ones were the offspring of whom, because the suckling of a lion cub does not indicate parenthood of that cub. I do not doubt, however, that lionesses can still recognize their own young, and vice versa.

Communal suckling also results in even more squabbling for nipples. Such squabbling starts early: I have heard the noises of it coming from very small cubs in their hiding place in a thicket with their radio-collared mother. Unlike some domestic kittens lion cubs do not apparently establish ownership of particular nipples, but all look for any nipple and try to push off a cub which is already suckling from one. The cub in possession resists, holding onto the nipple, making a high-pitched snarling noise, and trying to push away or swat the would-be usurper with a fore-paw. When cubs are being reared communally there are, of course, more competitors. I have seen a seething snarling mass of up to nine cubs all trying at the same time to get a meal from one of a lioness's four nipples. Not surprisingly she seems to find this uncomfortable, and after a while she bares her teeth, adds her own snarls to the chorus, and usually rolls over or moves off, so preventing all the cubs from feeding further.

Despite such squabbling over food, cubs are highly sociable towards all other members of the pride. They play with companions from their own litter or from other litters, indiscriminately as far as I could tell, and in ways which I have already described in Chapter 3. They play with adults too, who are extremely tolerant of the antics of small cubs;

86

this usually takes the form of chewing the tail tuft or climbing over the body of the resting adult. Sometimes the latter will bare its teeth at a cub, a very mild threat which warns it against coming too close; more often the adult moves away if reluctant to be played with. Cubs employ adults in other ways too, for apart from treating them as leaders, feeders and playthings, they use them as sunshades: if a group is out in the open without shade, small cubs can often be seen sheltering from the heat of the sun in the shadow cast by a large adult, particularly a male.

The cubs are fully dependent on milk for about the first three months of life, and their mothers usually stop lactating about six to eight months after giving birth. During the intervening period the cubs are being very gradually weaned, being able to get progressively less and less milk from adults, but obtaining an increasing proportion of their food from kills made by the adults. At first they do little more than lick blood, but soon they eat whatever meat they can obtain. When the cubs are less than about four months old, the adults go off hunting without them, one or two of their number and sometimes a male too, remaining with the cubs. If they catch a large enough prey animal, a lioness returns to the cubs and leads them all to the kill. When older than about four months, the cubs go with the lionesses everywhere, following behind on hunts.

Cubs grow quite fast, how fast depending particularly on how much

39 A lioness rests in TLFS posture, raising her chin as her four-month-old cub rubs himself against it

food they can get. A well-fed young lion of eighteen months can be almost the same size as an intermittently food-deprived one of two-and-a-half years, so I found it impossible to estimate a lion cub's age very accurately from its size. The sex is also difficult to determine before the cub is a few months old, when the scrotum of the males becomes clearly visible. From that time on, the cubs differ in other ways too. Males grow faster and have somewhat broader faces than females, and a few longer hairs begin to develop around the neck and betray their sex to the practised observer long before most people would recognize the beginnings of a mane. The black tuft begins to develop on the tip of the lengthening tail at about seven months, and the adult set of teeth come through at about fourteen months.

However, a great many, indeed most, lion cubs never reach that age. Cub mortality is high, which is a reflection of the fact that a lot of lion cubs are born. It is also very variable, depending partly on the conditions. At some times some prides rear most of their cubs while at other times other prides lose almost all of them. On average, though, I would estimate that between two-thirds and three-quarters of all lion cubs born do not survive to become adults. They are most vulnerable when they are very young, but are still apparently at risk until they are two years old; thereafter they are almost certain to reach adulthood.

In many cases I could not determine the cause of death. I would suddenly discover that a cub was no longer with its companions or with the adults when it was still too young to fend for itself, and I would never see it again thereafter. Some of these deaths may have been accidental, through a cub getting separated from its companions who then moved away without noticing its absence. Possibly some mothers are more careless than others in this respect. According to Judith Rudnai, a lioness might even abandon a single surviving cub if all the other cubs in its litter had died young; this would enable her to spend her time and energy on producing sooner a new litter with which she might be more successful. Disease claims the lives of some lion cubs, and so do accidents such as being drowned. Other cubs die violent deaths. Some may be gored or trampled by buffaloes; others are killed and perhaps eaten by leopards or hyaenas; more are killed by other lions, not regular pride members, who find them unprotected and treat them as defenceless strangers, rarely eating them.

Many cubs die partly or mainly of starvation. Of course, few animals which die slowly really die of a single cause: lion cubs which died of 'starvation' would in fact have succumbed to the combined effects of lack of food, cold, increased parasite loads and disease, or they may have been so weakened and slow that they did not avoid an aggressive buffalo quickly enough. Without finding their corpses, I attributed these cubs' deaths to starvation because they died at a time when they were very short of food; a single good meal at such a time might well have saved them (or, of course, it might only have delayed and prolonged their dying). A lion cub takes weeks to succumb to starvation, whereas another predator can kill it in seconds; any human observer is therefore much more likely to detect a cub dying of starvation than one dying between the teeth of another lion, for example. Thus we run into considerable difficulties when trying to determine the causes and extent of lion cub mortality.

Food supply certainly has a marked effect on cub survival. In the first two years of my study, the seasons were very pronounced: the dry seasons were long and completely dry, and abundant rain fell during the wet seasons. As a result the chief migratory prey species – zebra and wildebeest – spent long periods in the places where the grazing was best, and the lions in other areas had a lean time. The resident prides at the edge of the plains had to subsist on what gazelles they could catch during the dry seasons. At the same time the lions who lived in the woodlands were feasting on zebra and wildebeest; their difficult time came later, during the wet seasons when these two prey species were out on the plains, leaving the resident woodland lions to make a living mainly from impalas and warthogs. I have already described in Chapter 3 the competition which takes place at kills, and which is particularly intense when food is scarce and kills are small. Gazelles, impalas and warthogs are all really too small to be very good lion food – they do not provide enough to fill the stomachs of a whole group, let alone a whole pride. When the kills are small and there is competition for them, the cubs are the ones to suffer first, and most, because the dominance order at kills is based on prior possession and strength. Cub mortality was appreciably higher during those months when there were no large prey animals available in the resident lions' areas. These months were different for different prides; after all if the migratory species are not in one starving pride's area, they must be in the area of some other pride which is probably glutting itself with surplus food. In the last two years of my study the climate seemed to be more abnormal: some rain fell in the 'dry' season, and less during the wet season. The migratory prey species therefore moved about much more erratically, and were not absent from any parts of the park for such long periods. I think it was in consequence that lion cub survival during these two years was considerably better than in the two years preceding.

Food shortage affects cubs of all ages up to two years old, for during the whole of this time they are totally dependent on the adults to provide them with food. Larger cubs can of course survive periods of starvation better than smaller ones can, but they also need a greater quantity of food over a long period. Small cubs, on the other hand, can still get some of their food requirements from their mother's milk, and so are to some extent buffered and protected at that stage from the effects of a shortage of large prey animals.

I think it is now understandable why lions in East Africa do not have a birth season, as most animals do. Their day length does not alter greatly at different times of the year, because they live in the tropics, but nonetheless there are quite marked seasonal changes in the form of wet and dry seasons. These influence the breeding season of herbivores but not of lions. Why not? Being anthropomorphic for a moment: if I were a lioness trying to decide when was the best time to produce my cubs, I should be faced with enormous problems. I should have to think at least two years ahead, because my cubs would be dependent on me for that long. I might be able to guess roughly when during that time it would probably be dry and when wetter. I might even be able to do this moderately well for my own area, but hardly for other prides' areas too. Yet the distribution of rainfall and drought in different areas is what determines where and when the wildebeest will move. Even if my own area were completely bare and dry, prey animals might well pass through it in large numbers on their way to somewhere greener; even if my own area were green, other areas might be better still and hold the herbivores there. And even if I could make these almost impossible predictions, it would still be enormously difficult to calculate what age it would be best for my cubs to be to survive the lean periods I had predicted. In addition, all sorts of chance factors would upset my calculations: my failing to conceive, for example, or my cubs being killed by a hyaena, or my finding a newly dead elephant carcass which sustains my cubs at a critical time of food shortage. In the face of all these insoluble problems, what I should probably do is throw up my paws in horror and give up trying. I should decide to pay no attention to the time of year or the seasons but produce my cubs when I could, and just hope. This seems to be the course which lionesses have taken through natural selection over the generations, no longer timing their reproduction by environmental cues.

However, there are some important social cues to which lions do seem to pay attention. The synchronizing of births with other females in the pride is one of these. For the two prides for which I had most information, I calculated whether or for how long each litter of cubs survived. It turned out that litters which were born in synchrony with other litters in the same pride survived better than did litters which were born asynchronously. We can make a number of guesses at the probable reasons for this. The main reason seems to be that synchrony of births makes communal suckling and rearing possible. The cubs can get milk from other females who are also lactating, so they probably get a more regular milk supply and can feed when their own mother is not there. In addition, there is more likely to be a guardian near them: an adult, male or female, will often remain with the cubs of all the lionesses in the pride while the latter are hunting. Cubs need to be guarded, for hyaenas will kill and eat them, or buffaloes gore them if they come across them, but an adult lion with them can keep a hyaena away, and can lead cubs away from a buffalo. And partly, lions hunt together, and so must move around together. As their cubs get older, they move around more (and so became more difficult for me to find). It is presumably advantageous for each cub to be among others of the same age as itself, for if its companions were much older it would get left behind and would be late arriving at food, while if its companions were much younger they would probably hold it up in its movements in search for food. But if a female goes off on her own with her cubs, she can no longer benefit from communal hunting.

Another factor which may influence the chances of survival of lion cubs is whether there are older cubs present in the pride. In the prides I knew for longest, I found that new cubs were less likely to survive if the pride also contained cubs who were several months older. I guess that this was because the larger cubs were able to deprive the smaller cubs of food, both by arriving sooner at kills and by robbing them of pieces which the smaller cubs had managed to get hold of. The best strategy for a lioness to adopt is thus to produce her cubs when her companions do, a feat which probably requires some subtle signalling among lionesses.

SUBADULTS

Cubs which are fortunate enough to survive to two years old earn the title of subadults for the next year or so. If there are a batch of several of

40 A female cub of about eighteen months. She is in excellent condition. Her ears are undamaged, indicating that she has not been engaged in much competition for food. Her belly and hind limbs still bear clear juvenile spots

41 A male cub of about eighteen months, showing the first wisps of hair which will one day form a fine mane. Note the clear whisker spots and the uniformly pink muzzle of a young animal

them, and if they are the offspring of a fairly large pride, they are usually to be found in a group of their own, perhaps accompanied by one or two adult females. If there are only a couple of subadults, they tend to be better integrated with the rest of the pride, some of whose members will probably be rearing a later batch of offspring. At this stage lions are at their most inquisitive: it would almost always be a two-year-old male who would be the first of a group to come closer to examine my landrover, occasionally to test his teeth on my tyres (or was it vice versa?), and to trot after my car as I drove off.

Subadults also have to learn the difficult skill of hunting for themselves. One of the things it seems they need to learn is to curb their over-optimism: it is only subadults or large cubs who bother to run after an uncatchable zebra or a buffalo which has already seen them. They learn partly, no doubt, by trial and error the techniques of stalking, bringing down, and killing prey animals, but they probably benefit too from observing the methods of the more experienced adult lionesses with them.

During this learning period, the subadults are still within their own pride's area; although they may be moving around in it independently from most of the rest of the pride, they still meet them occasionally and amicably, although the young males give the adult males an increasingly wide berth. It is at the next stage of their lives that they may start to move further afield and to encounter hostile strange lions. The turning point in a lion's life – the point at which it leaves the pride if it is going to do so – comes when it is about three years old. The future paths of male and female lions diverge here. We will consider adult females first.

ADULT FEMALES

A three-year-old lioness looks full sized, but she is slimmer and lighter than an older adult. Her belly is taut, she is sleek and graceful, and she still bears the faint traces of her large juvenile spots on her limbs. Her canines are white and sharp pointed. She is moderately good at hunting, but will improve further with time.

Some young lionesses reaching the age of three remain in the pride for the rest of their adult lives, while others leave it, usually for ever. I found that the proportion of them that leave or remain depends on how large their pride is at the time. When the pride contains relatively few breeding adult lionesses, the subadult females are more likely to remain and so to boost its numbers. Conversely, when a pride is larger than it usually is, the subadults are more likely to depart. In this way a lion pride regulates its own size over the years: it prevents itself from growing too large, while it is more likely to increase when it is becoming too small.

I do not know what determines which subadults will stay and which will leave, nor really what makes them leave. They may go because they are driven out by the adults, but this is not a systematic expulsion; rather, a lioness may refuse to tolerate the presence of a particular subadult in her vicinity, and the subadult may therefore feel uneasy and eventually leave the pride's area semi-voluntarily. Lions probably have individual likes and dislikes, and we do not know what causes them. I have not found an instance of a lioness driving out her own daughter, and I think unfamiliarity between adults and subadults is likely to be important. The less well a lioness knows a subadult the more likely she is to be hostile towards her; the subadult then becomes more nervous, and this in turn makes her more likely to be attacked.

It is difficult to see why a subadult female should leave voluntarily, because life appears to be much more difficult for her once she has left her pride's area and taken up a nomadic existence. (The unenviable life of most nomadic lions is described in Chapter 5.) A lioness who has once left a pride and its area will not be allowed to rejoin it, and I know of no cases of strange females joining prides. Thus all the adult lionesses in a pride were born and reared there, and so are all related to one another.

A young lioness who is allowed to remain in her pride has a potentially rosy future. Her reproductive life typically starts when she is between three and four years of age with her first oestrous period, and in the Serengeti she produces her first litter of cubs when she is around four-and-a-half years old. In zoos and safari parks, and in areas where the lions have obtained an abundant and regular food supply, they grow faster and reproduce earlier; there is a record of a zoo lioness producing cubs when only twenty-four months old.

If a lioness's cubs die she generally comes into oestrus again within a few months, and then produces a new litter about nine months after the death of the last cub of her previous litter. Since cubs can die at any age, this obviously produces an irregular spacing between births. If, on the other hand, she is more successful or fortunate in rearing her cubs, she does not usually come into oestrus until the surviving cubs are about a year-and-a-half old, and produces her next litter when they are about two years old. Thus a successful female produces cubs at about two-yearly intervals, while a very unsuccessful one whose cubs always die would give birth every year. I do not know what prevents a lioness coming into oestrus when her cubs are younger. I never saw a lactating lioness mating; milk production probably inhibits the oestrous cycle in lionesses, as it does in many mammals and to some extent in humans. However, since a lioness has stopped producing milk by the time her cubs are nine months yet does not come into oestrus for a further nine months, there must be some other mechanism by which the presence of her cubs shuts off any oestrous behaviour. One lioness who deserted her two cubs, leaving them in the care of a companion who also had young, produced her next litter only seventeen months after her previous one, the shortest interval I observed between litters by a female whose cubs were still alive.

Barring accidents, a typical lioness's life continues along this steady path for years. She produces cubs. If they die, she produces a new litter about nine months after their death. If one or more of them survive, she produces her next litter when she has reared them to the age of about two years. With time she looks older too. Her teeth change, as I have described in Chapter 2, and through the actions of biting flies and squabbling lion claws, her ears become more notched or tattered, and often rather bare of fur. Her fur gets slightly darker with age, her eyes look more sunken, her nose, particularly, more scarred, and her gait heavier. Even walking looked to me to be more of an effort for an elderly lioness than for a younger one. She continues to produce cubs at intervals until within a couple of years of her death. Very old females are not driven out; they remain full members of their pride until their death, even when they are no longer producing cubs or contributing usefully to the pride's hunting efforts.

It is difficult to tell how long lions usually live in the wild – we have not been observing known individuals for long enough. However, I have used a couple of other methods of estimating their average longevity. About half of the individually known lionesses in two prides at Seronera were no longer alive there after a period of six years had elapsed, but had been replaced by younger females. This suggests that all would probably have died by the time twice as long had elapsed, indicating a rough average of twelve years of adult life; with three years as a cub and then subadult, we get an average lifespan of around fifteen years for a lioness who remains in her pride as an adult. Another way by which I reached a similar figure was by observing the teeth of animals of known age and by recording the changes in the teeth of all known lions over the four years I was studying them. This figure of fifteen years is the probable figure for adult females, although some may, of course, live considerably longer than that. In zoos, the oldest lions recorded died at the age of about thirty. Such maximum figures tend to be more publicized than those for all the lions who died younger, and I do not know the average age at which captives die. I should be very surprised if a lioness in the wild were to live to be as old as thirty. After all, she has to cope with parasites and disease sapping her strength, to get through periodic times of food shortage, to overcome the effects of wounds and of teeth broken in encounters with hostile lions and with prey animals, and to travel considerable distances while doing so. By contrast a zoo lion, supplied with abundant food, kept free of parasites and deprived of the opportunity to wear herself out, would be expected to live considerably longer; boredom is rarely lethal.

ADULT MALES

The male lion's path through life is rather different from that of the female's. At about three years old all subadult males leave the pride in which they were born and reared. As with the subadult females which left, I could not really tell why they were going – whether they were driven out by the adults or whether they left of their own accord because there was little future for them in their own pride – though I suspect mainly the former. They are capable of mating, but rarely do so because an oestrous female in their pride mates with one of the adult males, not with one of the subadults which she may well have helped to rear. At this stage these young males are larger than adult females but still not quite as heavy as full-grown males. Their fur is beginning to change from the brown colour of females and cubs to the slightly greyer tint of adult males. Their manes vary, and indeed the size of the mane is not a good measure of the age of a lion. A subadult usually has quite long pale hairs around his neck; these do not extend right up onto the top of his head as in an adult, and so he often has a rather 'washed-behind-the-ears' appearance. His mane at this age does not stretch far back either, merely projecting slightly above his shoulders.

The young males leave the pride and its area together, and stay together as a group as they move around for a couple of years following the wandering life of nomads. They travel where food is easiest to come by, and no longer confine themselves to a single area. They hunt

1   The golden head of an adult male lion in golden grass

2 Three cubs of different ages at a milk source

3 My young radio-collared female leopard

4   A young leopard rolls playfully on his back

5   Congestion, as many lion cubs cross a stream by means of a fallen tree

6 A cheetah with her four cubs which are only just old enough to have emerged into the open

7 I weigh an immobilized lioness on a platform balanced on two sets of bathroom scales

together, not yet having acquired the huge mane which presumably hinders the hunting efforts of a fully adult male by making him conspicuous. They also scavenge to a large extent, from the carcasses of animals which have died of natural causes or which have been killed by hyaenas or other lions. Their being in a group helps them to compete with other rival groups of lions or with packs of hyaenas better than any of them could alone.

I do not really know where they go during this period, nor how large a distance they cover. Once a group of young males had left the pride's area in which they grew up I rarely saw them again. On the few occasions when I did, they were back in that same area. I think, therefore, that they probably range quite widely, but that in the course of their travels they pass through the familiar region of their youth and use it as a slightly more peaceful place in which to spend some time. Perhaps their parents and relatives chase and harry them on their way less than do the other resident prides through whose territories they have to travel.

After a couple of years, the group of young males may be able to become resident pride males themselves, by taking over a pride and its area. There are a number of different ways in which they may manage to do this. Sometimes they can find a pride where the previous adult

42 Three subadult males with still-embryonic manes rest in an inadequate patch of shade

males have died, been killed or left. Sometimes, by virtue of their superior strength or their greater numbers, they can drive out the resident males; the latter probably have a reasonable idea of what fights they might be able to win and when it would be better to leave than to lose. Sometimes, though, there are fierce fights, as I describe in Chapter 5. Pride takeovers are not sudden affairs. Usually the new males settle at the edge of the pride's area for a few weeks, or even longer, before managing to extend their activities across it. Then one day I would find those new males with the females, perhaps mating with them or feeding at the same kill, in the middle of the pride's area, where previously the resident males would never have allowed them. I then considered the takeover to be complete. The group of new males thus start on the reproductive phase of their adult life, for which possession of a pride is essential.

The pride they now own is very unlikely to be the one in which they grew up, although that may very occasionally occur. Thus the males are not related closely, if at all, to the females in the pride they have taken over, so little inbreeding takes place. But we can see why the breeding adult males in a pride *are* likely to be quite closely related to one another: they are the offspring of sometimes one but usually several related females in a pride, and they have grown up together and subsequently stayed together as a group of companions-cum-relatives until their takeover of a different pride. If I have stressed these points about relatedness too often, it is because I consider them to be the fundamental cornerstones of lion society. Until years more of research has been done it is impossible to say how much the males usually disperse from their birthplace: I think they are a bit more likely to settle eventually somewhere near the area in which they were reared.

The takeover of a pride, the launching of the new males' breeding life, causes a major upheaval in that of the females in the pride they have taken over. At first the lionesses who have cubs tend to avoid the newly arrived males. They have good cause to do so because those newcoming males are liable at first to kill some of the cubs they come across. They sometimes, but rarely, eat the cubs they have killed, and I discuss in Chapter 10 their evolutionary 'motives' for this exceedingly anti-social behaviour, which at first surprised me greatly. I found it difficult to tell how often this cub-killing occurs. The corpse of one killed cub I examined had just one neat pair of holes where a male's canine teeth had crushed its shoulders and backbone: one bite and two shakes had been enough to kill it. I found the carcass in the long grass only because the radio-collared male responsible was still carrying it around with him when I tracked him. Usually the corpse would have been left and my chances of discovering it would have been minute. Therefore the fact that I recorded four such instances implies that there must have been many more which I knew nothing about, but I do not know how many more. Certainly the new males do not indulge in a wholesale slaughter of cubs, but on the other hand the takeover of a pride does result in an increase in the mortality of cubs of any age in that pride. Some of these deaths may be only indirectly due to the new males. Possibly, for example, their presence causes stress for the lionesses who therefore hunt less efficiently, or produce less milk, or waste time and effort trying in vain to guard their cubs; I discuss in Chapter 10 why they cannot be completely successful at protecting their young.

Apart from the new males' rather dramatic effects on cubs which have already been born, they also apparently have an influence on when the females will give birth next. I found that after new males gain possession of a pride, there is generally an interval of a few months during which almost no litters of cubs are born. This slack period is then followed by a 'baby boom', a burst in cub production about eight months after their takeover. The causes of this unevenness in the birth rate are not clear, although I discuss the possible reasons later, again in Chapter 10.

Once the new males have been in possession for a few months, pride life is back to normal again. The males tend more often to be found in the company of the lionesses, and they no longer represent any danger to the cubs. They feed mainly on kills made by the females, and they stick to and mate with any lioness in the pride who may come into oestrus. This occupies a fairly large proportion of their time, nearly one-fifth for the males I radio-tracked! After all, the adult females in a pride outnumber the males by two or three to one, they come into oestrus quite often because of the low success rate, and when in heat they mate very frequently. I calculated that a typical successful adult male lion might well mate roughly 20,000 times during his lifetime.

Apart from this fairly strenuous performance, pride life is hard work for males in other ways too, despite no longer needing to hunt for themselves. The adult males travel further than the females do, crossing and patrolling their group territory, marking it and expelling intruders. Some large groups of males manage subsequently to take over an adjacent pride as well, and to be in possession of both concurrently. One group of six males owned three prides, and then it was only by having them radio-collared that I could find some of them in the large area they were covering. Each would be sometimes with one or more of his companions and sometimes alone; on some days with one pride and on other days with a different one; sometimes mating and sometimes with a kill.

Such a life cannot continue indefinitely. Males age quite fast. After a few years have elapsed, accidents, injuries and disease have together reduced both the number of males in the group and their strength. All the time there is likely to be pressure from groups of younger males trying to find a pride to take over. In the Serengeti, where such pressure seems to be particularly strong, a pair of males manages to retain possession of a pride for only two to three years on average before being expelled. Except for one particularly large male who owned a small pride and small territory on his own for over a year, no other adult male retained possession of a pride single-handed for more than two or three months. As I describe in the next chapter, two males fighting co-operatively can usually defeat a singleton. This is one of the great advantages for males of having companions. Groups of three or more males kept ownership of prides for much longer than pairs of males could, and also sometimes took over adjacent prides too. Therefore large groups of males fathered many more offspring than did smaller groups.

On the whole, because males did not remain in possession of prides for more than a few years, incest rarely occurred. If a young lioness comes into oestrus first at about three-and-a-half years old, her own father is unlikely to be still around to mate with her then. He might be, if he is one of a large and therefore long-lasting group; but in that case the male with whom the young lioness mates is more likely just by chance to be one of his companions rather than her father.

Eventually, however, any male's tenure of a pride must end. He is expelled, perhaps after a fight, by stronger males, and his only option is to become nomadic again, as he was for a while when he was about four years old. Now, though, at the age of perhaps ten, life is much more difficult for him. He may well be on his own, in which case he can no longer hunt co-operatively. Alone he is less able to compete against the other scavengers. His size, his mane, his blunted teeth, his slowness with age all make solitary hunting even more of a problem than it was before. He may have been injured during his expulsion, and now he probably receives further wounds when trying to get food. Lack of food,

43 A very old male. His canine teeth are worn down to blunt stubs, and he has lost almost all his incisors. His face looks gaunt and his ribs form corrugations through the skin of his chest. Ousted from his pride, he is gradually dying of starvation

combined with disease, probably kill him within a year or two of his expulsion, perhaps with hyaenas assisting the very last stages of the process. One very old dying male I came across was a pitiful sight. His brownish canine teeth were worn down to the gum, clearly visible as his lower jaw drooped and his breath clicked. I could see almost every bone in his body, as all his flesh seemed to have wasted away, leaving a skeleton tightly covered with scarred skin. Although a pathetic spectacle, his very age meant that he had probably had an unusually successful life.

As in our own species, male lions generally die younger than females, partly I think because they wear themselves out, and partly because they are deprived of the benefits of pride life when expelled. A lion without a pride is out of its proper habitat. A male's effective reproductive period is much shorter than that of a lioness. It will have been much busier, though, and in the few brief years that he was in joint possession of a pride a male lion will have fathered more than enough offspring to replace him and to continue the lion's life cycle.

5 · Lion territories and land use

A lion-watcher soon notices that lions have definite ranges within which they spend almost all their time. Whenever I found a particular lion – if I managed to find it – it was within such a range. Not only did I tend to find the same lions there, but I found other lions not there. Lions' ranges are largely exclusive, and thus they merit the term 'territory', for the word means an area of ground which is 'owned' by an animal who prevents or deters other animals of the same species from entering or settling there.

Lions' territories are more complicated because they are group territories, owned communally. The members of a pride do not necessarily all move around together in their joint territory, but individually or collectively they all make use of roughly the same area. The adult females in a pride will have spent almost every hour of their whole lives within that range. This 'faithfulness' to an area was a great help when I started studying lions: it meant that I could soon learn which lions I was more likely to meet where, and this made those individuals easier to recognize, and also rendered slightly less arduous the job of finding particular animals. However, one cannot absolutely guarantee that a lion will always be in its territory, because it may just occasionally go off on a 'trip'. An example was an elderly lioness in the small pride of four females in whose territory my hovel was situated. I had her radio-collared for nearly two years, during which time I could be sure of finding her whenever I wanted. She and her companions were always within an area four to five miles across – except once when eventually I found her alone far further away, about five miles beyond the edge of their area. She was back in her pride's territory again the next day, and I never discovered the reason for her excursion. Nor would I ever have known about it had I not been radio-tracking her: I would merely have assumed that my failure to find her that day was because she was either in cover or in some part of her range which I had not searched. I must stress, however, that this trip was highly exceptional, and that lions are almost always inside their territories.

Lions do not necessarily use the whole of their territory evenly. The larger prides in my study area tended to be subdivided into two or more smaller subgroupings of a few females and cubs, and these subdivisions lasted for a long time. The different subgroups tended to concentrate their activities in different parts of the whole pride's territory, and as a result they met one another less than if they had all used the whole area more evenly. When they did meet they interacted peacefully, and clearly they still belonged to the same pride. It is likely that sometimes these subgroups could become more and more isolated from one another in different parts of the territory. They might then encounter the other subgroups so rarely that they behaved towards them in a hostile manner, and thus a large pride with a large range would effectively have split into two new prides, each with its own smaller territory. I have some evidence of this process happening.

As we have seen, the female line in the pride is permanent, and the group of lionesses occupies the same area from one generation to the next, barring accidents. The males, on the other hand, change from time to time. When a new pair or group of males takes over a pride, they also acquire ownership over the territory of the resident members of that pride; and when larger groups of males sometimes manage to keep possession of two prides concurrently, the females in each pride still retain their same pride territories and exclude any other females who intrude into their range. Although the groups of males in these cases control a much larger area, I think it is more useful to think of the position in terms of their owning two distinct territories rather than a territory larger than that of the lionesses.

These lion territories do not have precise boundaries. On a map I could, of course, draw a line joining all the outermost points where I saw a particular lion or pride, but this outer line is fairly arbitrary. If the apparent edges of their ranges are drawn onto a landscape map, they rarely correspond with any geographical features. The range of one pride in my study area was bounded by a high ridge, which the lions went up onto but not past, but otherwise the most peripheral points at which I saw particular lions did not lie along river banks, hilltops or woodland edges. Instead the edges seemed to depend on where the edges of their neighbours' territories were. I found that the zone between adjacent prides tended to be less intensively used than the rest of the prides' areas, and thus it was as though there was a kind of no-man's-land or buffer zone between neighbouring prides. Although the animals from either pride might be found within this zone, it was on the whole unlikely that they would be. Lions tend to avoid their neighbours, and usually they stay clear of those neighbours' land, although they may transgress more when they are finding it difficult to get enough food within their own territory.

In areas such as the woodlands of the Serengeti where I worked and where resident prey animals are available throughout the year, the system I have just outlined seems to be the normal pattern. By contrast, George Schaller described other Serengeti lion ranges as overlapping extensively. However, he was working at Seronera, at the woodlands-plains edge, where the lion territories altered according to the season of the year. In the dry season, the prides living there occupy territories at the edge of the woodlands, while the parched plains to the east of them are largely devoid of possible prey animals except for occasional gazelles and ostriches and so are virtually uninhabitable for lions. Then, when the wet season comes, the huge migratory populations of wildebeest and zebras move out of the woodlands and onto the short green grass of the open plains. From being a dry, dusty, empty desert, useless as far as lions are concerned, the area becomes a fruitful place for hunting adundant prey animals, and so the prides living around the edges all tend to shift their territories eastwards and take advantage of the feeding opportunities there. The positions of these territories relative to one another stay much the same, and at any one season there is little overlap. It is only if one plots the positions of different prides throughout the yearly cycle that their ranges appear to overlap. By analogy, the two windscreen wipers on my car cover most of the same area over the course of each cycle, yet they are never close to one another; they have similarly shifting areas of influence. Lions are adaptable animals, and their territorial system is flexible and modified according to local needs.

Territories vary in size, but do not seem to change in size much with time. Where there are ample numbers of resident prey animals, a pride usually occupies between ten and forty square miles. Larger prides tend to have larger areas, but I do not know which causes which. It seems likely that a large pride in a small range would gradually manage to appropriate some of its neighbours' range. It is possible, too, that some territories have to be larger than others in order to ensure that there will be some unpredictable food available somewhere within them at all times of the year; if so, the larger territory can support more lions, so the pride could afford to allow its numbers to grow more by not expelling so many subadult females.

USE OF TERRITORY

How lions move around in their range depends on many factors, some of which we know and many of which we do not. The distribution of the different kinds of resources in the particular territory is important. For example in some there is a shortage of suitable places in which to spend the day – such as good shady trees, or kopjes, or dry river beds where the lions may obtain shade and seclusion. In such areas, lions tend to return to the same few daytime resting places at the end of their night forays over the surrounding area. One pride containing radio-collared females I tracked was usually to be found by day somewhere along a one-mile stretch of river, and therefore it appeared at first sight to use a rather small area. Yet when I tracked them at night and over a longer period they proved to be moving over a much larger area of about twenty square miles.

Knowledge of any favoured daytime resting places made it considerably easier to find particular lions – when they were there. Many prides or individuals, though, do not seem to show similar preferences for particular places. These lions might be anywhere in their territory, by day or night, which makes them more interesting, though more difficult to find. How far they go depends particularly on how many potential prey animals there are around. If lions can catch prey without going long distances, they may stay in much the same place for days. One group I was watching spent at least a fortnight close to a river crossing-point where they were successfully catching victims from migrating wildebeest herds. If prey are less abundant, lions have to go further to find them, and in that case they move around their territory more extensively. Another factor which limits lions' movements is small cubs; until these are reasonably mobile, at about four months old, their presence tends to restrict their mothers' movements.

We can look at the use of lion territories in another sense, namely of the functions they serve. In considering the question 'Why do lions have territories?', we should recognize the fact that there are two distinct aspects of the question. First, why do lions confine themselves to the same area, and second, why do they exclude other lions from that area? There must be a number of advantages in staying in one area rather than moving haphazardly over an enormous range, one of the main advantages to a lion probably being that it can learn all about that area. It will know where it can find water, for example, and the good places for hunting. In the same way, I too found knowledge of my study area was a tremendous help, in enabling me to go straight to places where I could cross rivers, or could see a long way, or to avoid places which were seething with maddening tsetse flies. A lion can also regain contact with its companions if they all remain within the same range. The lion's flexible system whereby the pride members meet and disperse, moving about together or alone, is only possible if all members stay in the same restricted area. The obvious disadvantage of staying there is that the food supply may not do the same, which is why lion pride territories are established only where there are enough prey animals within the area throughout the year.

Presumably there are advantages in keeping other lions out of the territory: they might compete for food, or disturb prey animals which the owners were hunting. They might also harm vulnerable members of the pride, such as the cubs. Keeping out all intruders completely is obviously impossible over an area of dozens of square miles, nor is it absolutely necessary. But by driving out intruders whenever they are encountered, the resident pride can ensure that no other pride manages to settle permanently in their territory and offer any serious competition.

MAINTENANCE AND DEFENCE OF THE TERRITORY

The main way in which resident lions deter others from trying to settle in their territory is by making it clear that the area is already occupied. This they do by roaring, urine-marking and patrolling their territory.

Roaring I have already mentioned in Chapter 3. The roar is a magnificently impressive noise, of tremendous volume, and the sound of lions roaring nearby at night was always a delight to me. A group of females and cubs would be lying inactive, scattered around near my

44 A pair of lions roars in synchrony, pushing forward their noses with the effort of forcing out each roar

landrover in the newly crept-in darkness, a slight paleness of their lower flanks betraying their positions in the starlight. Through the shrilling of the crickets and the warm 'korrr' calls of the little scops owl would come first a low sad-sounding moan, then another louder one, and then following at about two-second intervals a whole succession of remarkably pure-toned powerful roars. From close quarters I could hear the straining in the throat of the 'singer' as each roar began. By the time the first lioness's roars were fading away into a long series of gruff throaty grunts, some of her companions would have joined in too, the whole powerful chorus sending vibrations through my landrover. Within a minute or two after the last lion had become silent again, I would often hear an answering chorus from a neighbouring pride a couple of miles or more away. An intruding lion would be left in little doubt that the area he or she was in was already claimed by a number of resident lions. He does not reply, and if the owners are close he will often move away at the sound of their roaring. Pride males roar somewhat more often than females, particularly while they are patrolling their territories.

The second method of proclaiming a territory is by marking it with the smell of the owners' urine. This urine-marking is done much more

45 Before scent-marking a bush, a male sniffs at the branches and rubs his mane against them

46 A male sprays urine onto a bush, holding his tail vertically

by males than by females, and is of two distinct forms. One type sprays the vegetation. The lion approaches a bush or small tree which has twigs at head height. He sniffs at the leaves for a few seconds, then briefly rubs his head through them before moving on or turning his body so as to bring his rear close to them; then with his tail held high he projects urine in a series of powerful sprays onto the vegetation. Mixed with the urine are secretions from the anal glands which impart a powerful odour to it. The trees chosen tend to be reused by him as well as by other lions, and may act as an olfactory noticeboard; they presumably indicate who has been there and how recently. Unfortunately human noses such as mine are nowhere near as sensitive as lions', and I could not gather this kind of information. The other type of urine-marking is by squirting urine onto the hind feet as they are scraped alternately on the ground. This is a less conspicuous but more common form of marking. It probably helps the lion both to mark that particular spot and also to leave a trail of his scented footprints wherever he goes. Therefore as a result of lions' movements around their territory, the whole area is likely to acquire a faint but definite odour of its owners.

Males cross and re-cross their territory in the course of their patrolling. They may be together or alone. They do not take an organized route, but seem to move rather unpredictably, responding to what stimuli they encounter. They may hear other pride members feeding at a kill, for example, or detect and follow the trail of a female in oestrus. They may also detect intruders and drive them off if they come across them. Sometimes when I played a strange male lion's roars from a tape-recorder to a resident pride male, the latter would adopt a superb aggressive posture with the head held high and rigid as he advanced in the direction of the noises and went on past my car, roaring at intervals as he went. Sometimes, however, he took no apparent notice of the noise; I presume that either he considered the 'intruder' to be no immediate threat, or else he could detect the inadequacies of my recording and playback system.

INTERACTIONS WITH INTRUDERS

There are different categories of intruding lions, and the resident lions' reactions to these vary according to the different kinds of threat or competition they offer.

Territorial clashes with neighbouring prides are rare. It appears that each pride knows the limits of its own territory and very roughly respects them. When the females of different prides do encounter one another it tends to be at the edges of their ranges, and the groups are likely to try to avoid one another. Both appear to be somewhat uneasy, and after possibly a brief skirmish they each return towards their own areas. Although the territory boundaries are not at all sharply defined, they do seem to be fairly well recognized, and to provoke few disputes. If a single animal of one pride is encountered in their territory by a group of a neighbouring pride, he or she usually flees and is chased, driven, or escorted out. It is clearly noticeable that, as George Schaller described, the pursuer appears reluctant to catch the intruder, and both animals usually slow to a walking pace. It is probably better to drive out an intruder gently than to risk injury to oneself in expelling it more violently.

As I described, if an intruding female is in oestrus, a resident pride male does not drive her out but is willing to mate with her, and similarly a resident oestrous female who encounters a nomadic male is prepared to mate with him. In general, even if no animals are in oestrus, each sex tends to be less intolerant towards intruders of the opposite sex. To a resident pride male, an intruder represents a threat to his food supply and to the safety of his offspring; but in addition, if the intruder is a male, it may also threaten his tenure of his pride.

Fights with casual intruders do not often result in serious injury. There is a considerable amount of snarling and swatting, but usually the intruder manages to escape just with scratches on its nose and hindquarters. Fights between rival males are much more serious, and may well result in death. These occur when a new group of males attempts to take over a pride by ousting the males already in possession. In any such fight, numbers are important. Two lions are likely to be able to defeat a single one, which therefore usually gives way. This does not mean that he is automatically ousted. If he is a pride male who has one or more companions elsewhere, he can rejoin them and later they may be able to scare off or defeat the challengers together.

Lions fight co-operatively. A lion on his own is in trouble against more than one other because his rear end is vulnerable to a second opponent while he is attacking a first. Females lack the size and strength of males, and the protective mane, but they can sometimes put a male to flight by their greater numbers. This happened to one of a pair of males in the early stages of their eventual takeover of a pride I was watching. This pride had only a single adult male at that stage, the

47 An adult male with a fully developed mane, dark, conspicuous, protective and intimidating

other having disappeared a few weeks earlier. The two intruding males, who had been established at the edge of the pride's area for a few months, watched from a kopje the large pride filing past, strung out in a long line with the cubs and the male at the rear. Then they started to follow stealthily and gradually gained on the resident male. He eventually noticed them coming and immediately started to trot away, chased by the two assailants. But while the cubs scattered and fled, the nine females ran back and surrounded one of the intruding males. Whenever he tried to flee the females chased him, biting at his haunches and so forcing him to stop and turn to defend his rear end. Finally, he was chased and then driven a few hundred yards away by the females, while his companion was doing the same to the pride male. The conflict was clearly inconclusive on this occasion. Nonetheless the intruders later managed to take over the pride completely, and the resident male disappeared. Without his companion he could not retain possession even with the help of the lionesses.

Fights do not usually last long. The claws of the forepaws rake at any part of the opponent's body they can reach, and this often results in large tufts of mane being torn out. The sharp canine teeth, just over two inches long, strike into an exposed part of the anatomy of the loser – the rump or neck particularly – and can do a considerable amount of damage. How much damage I saw one night when I came across a male defeated in a fight. He was completely paralysed in the hindquarters by a bite in his spine, but otherwise there were few wounds except superficial scratches on either him or his conqueror. The latter was walking up and down near him, roaring often, and occasionally coming close enough for them to exchange a few swats, but not attacking further. To do so would have been unnecessary, for the injured lion was completely defeated and was dead within thirty-six hours.

NOMADIC LIONS

So far in this book I have been concerned with resident lions, which make up the great successful majority of the Serengeti lion population. However, a minority of lions – about one-sixth of them – do not remain as residents within circumscribed small areas but move nomadically over far larger ranges. These lions do not look any different from residents, and when occasionally I encountered a small group of strange lions in the middle of my study area I would guess that they were nomads rather than residents only because I had never seen them before and would probably never see them again. George Schaller studied nomadic lions when they were out on the open plains, where nomadic lions are commoner than in my woodland area, and his work provides most of the information in this section.

The nomads of the lion population are those animals who have been expelled from the resident prides in the woodlands. Many of them are young males who have left or been driven from the pride in which they were born, and who are not yet old and strong enough to take over another resident pride as breeding adults. A nomadic spell lasting for a year or two is a normal part of the life history of all males, both successful and unsuccessful ones. The rest of the nomads, though, tend to be the unsuccessful, the old and the outcasts. Some of these are fully adult males who have probably never managed to take over a pride, but who still might, if they are fortunate. A few are old males who have been ousted from the pride of which they were in possession, and who will probably die fairly soon. And some are females who are the surplus from successful resident prides which reared more young females than were needed to replace losses, and who were expelled as subadults instead of being recruited into those prides as breeding adults.

113

48 Two nomadic subadult males pace in step across the open expanse of the Serengeti plains

With no ties to a particular piece of land, the nomads go wherever food is available. In the Serengeti this means that they tend to follow the enormous herds of migratory wildebeest, zebras and gazelles. During the wet season these herds are out on the open grass plains, which are teeming with potential prey but not with lions because the country is not suitable year-round lion habitat. On the plains there are no resident prides to chivy the nomads. Some of the latter try to set up temporary territories on the plains, but this appears to involve a great deal of work for very little gain, and most move more haphazardly. Although prey animals are more difficult to stalk close to or ambush on the flat plains than in the more concealing woodland where I worked, there are a great many more of these potential prey so there are much better chances of finding dead, dying, sick or slow ones. A larger proportion of nomads' food than of residents' food is from scavenging, feeding from carcasses of animals which have died of disease or old age, or which have been killed by hyaenas, the other main predator-cum-scavenger which is common in such open country. By contrast hyaenas were scarce in my area.

With a fair number of nomadic lions moving around the plains, encounters among them are frequent. Nomadic lions tend to be more tolerant of strangers than resident pride animals are, perhaps because they are not as unknown to the lions concerned as we think. They may not behave amicably towards all other nomads, but they probably recognize them from past encounters. A nomad is quite likely to allow another nomad to feed from its kill; by contrast, a pride member would not allow a nomad or a member of another pride to share its food. Although they may have one or two firm companions, the nomads do not form stable groups. They are not just normal lions who do not happen to restrict their movements to the confines of a territory; they are lions who are unable to establish the complex social system of most successful lions. Such a social system seems to require a permanent area within which to operate.

At the end of the wet season, the migratory prey leave the plains and disperse into the woodlands, and the nomadic lions do the same. There they find themselves in the territories of resident prides who do not allow them to settle. Nomads probably move as much as they do because they are encouraged to do so by hostile territorial residents. This does not happen all the time, for there is enough space in a lion pride's territory for nomadic intruders to remain undetected or undisturbed for days or weeks, but eventually they will have to move on again. Thus the total area traversed by a nomadic lion in the course of its lifetime in the Serengeti is probably a few thousand square miles, far greater than for a resident.

In addition the lifetime of a nomad, male or female, is usually shorter than that of a resident. Without a stable pride to assist and support him or her, a nomad probably finds it more difficult to get enough food, and has to put in more effort to get it. It has to travel long distances, and it finds itself involved in many hostile encounters with better-fed residents. It may stray outside the protection of a national park, and there fall victim to a human's snare or rifle. An example of this was when Schaller was sent the ear-tag which he had long before put onto a nomadic male, an animal which ended its life to flatter a sport hunter's vanity.

Nomadic females produce fewer cubs than do resident lionesses, and the survival chances of those few are lower. Hyaenas and strange lions are much more abundant, and either will kill cubs they come upon. It is difficult for a nomadic lioness to get her cubs fed, for the numerous other scavengers make short work of a carcass if she leaves it unguarded while she fetches her cubs, and she is unlikely to have companions who will guard either her cubs or her kill for her. It is difficult for any carnivore to be as mobile as the hoofed prey on which it feeds, and lion cubs particularly are not adapted to follow the extensive movements of such an inveterate traveller as the wildebeest.

Nomadic lionesses thus tend to be unsuccessful. We may wonder

115

why, then, they become nomadic. The answer is probably that they have little choice in the matter, because a pride can expel its surplus subadult females. If they are driven out of their pride and so lose all the advantages of pride life, the best option left open to them is to go where the food appears to be most available, and this usually means becoming nomadic. If these lionesses should find an area where they can settle permanently they will probably do so, and thus found a new pride. This must sometimes happen, for with natural changes in the environment some unsuitable areas may become suitable for permanent occupation by lions. Also some established prides may die out, or become weak and be unable to prevent newcomers from settling permanently in part of their area. Nonetheless, such opportunities are probably rare, and the average nomadic lioness's life is likely to be relatively short, strenuous, and unproductive.

49 A young lioness, recently embarked on a nomadic way of life. Nomads produce fewer cubs than do residents, rear even fewer and have relatively short lives

6 · Predation

HUNTING METHODS

Lions are carnivores: they feed on meat and are specialized for the process of catching, killing and consuming that meat. Prey animals, however, the source of the meat, are adapted for avoiding being caught, so they are generally alert and speedy. It is important to bear in mind this conflict in adaptations when we consider hunting by lions.

Like other cats, lions can accelerate very quickly and can run fast, up to about thirty or thirty-five miles per hour, but as cats they are not good long distance runners and they cannot keep up this speed for more than about 100–200 yards. Almost all their prey animals can run faster than lions can, and can keep it up for longer; I have seen even a warthog outpace a lioness. Thus the basic problem for a lion is how to get close enough to a potential prey animal to be able to sprint and capture it, before the prey has started running away fast enough to escape. There are two possible ways of getting close to a distant animal: to go towards it, or to wait in case it comes towards you. Most lion hunts are a combination of these two methods of reducing distance, stalking and ambushing.

It is obvious to a lion-watcher that during the daytime lions first detect their prey by seeing or sometimes by hearing them; at night, when visibility is reduced, hearing becomes relatively more important. Lions' sense of smell is probably of little help in finding live animals, except perhaps in very thick vegetation. Having seen potential prey, the lion usually watches it for a while in an alert posture, and then starts to approach it. She (for it is usually a lioness) may walk or trot towards distant prey if there is little likelihood of being detected. As she gets closer she adopts a stalking posture: her head is held low, her legs are

50 A lioness, having seen an opportunity, runs semi-stalking towards a potential victim

51 Motionless in sphinxed posture, a lioness watches for an opportunity to stalk nearer to a group of grazing wildebeest; all of them can run faster than she can, so she has to stalk to within very close range of them

bent, and her whole body is tense. She can move fast when the prey is looking away; at other times she can remain completely statue-like, either crouched or with her stomach just off the ground. All the time she watches the behaviour of her intended meal. Throughout her hunting, her expression is an alert, not an aggressive one. She is merely trying in a businesslike way to feed, and she feels no more aggression towards the prey she is planning to attack than that prey does towards the grass it is eating or than you or I do towards our dinner. She merely has to be more skilled in how she approaches it. She is adept at using any cover there may be to assist her in her stalking: streams, tree-trunks, thickets, even small clumps of grass. She is patient, sometimes excessively so I thought, and may wait beside a patch of cover for minutes on end, particularly if the prey is very alert or moving towards her. There is naturally an element of ambush in a stalk. Sometimes a lion will conceal itself near a waterhole where it knows that prey animals will come, and where it can ambush them. Sometimes it sees prey travelling, and stalks to hide itself in a position to intercept them.

The potential prey animal is meanwhile going about its business. It is unaware of the presence of a predator nearby, but nonetheless it is alert. If grazing, it raises its head at intervals and looks around. It keeps an eye on its companions and is sensitive to any changes of behaviour on their part. It avoids patches of cover or approaches them with caution. It is ready to flee at any suspicious sound, smell or movement. Most ungulates have good general purpose vision which covers a wide angle and is sensitive to movement and at night, but their eyesight is probably not particularly acute for motionless objects, and they cannot see colour. No eye can do everything well. It is well known that lions' coats blend well with the colour of dried grass; indeed I have had surprise encounters with lions whom I had not noticed in a clump of long golden grass stems. Once it was only after several minutes of scanning the distance with binoculars from the roof of my car that I discovered that the lion who was the object of my search was in fact lying just a few yards away, concealed only by his colour, and puzzled I think by my behaviour. But to remain undetected by an ungulate, which can only see in black and white, perfect colour matching is superfluous. It is enough that the tawny coat of a lion is neither very bright nor very dark, and is therefore inconspicuous against most backgrounds. Movement would betray a lion's presence much more, and lions are expert at moving stealthily when the prey animal is not looking.

Usually the approaching lion does not manage to get within range of the prey. Often I saw the intended victim move away, completely unaware of the lion's presence. Sometimes it may detect a movement by the predator, or its smell. If it does, it starts suddenly and flees swiftly to a safer place, away from cover, where it can look about it. From there, usually only about a hundred yards away, it utters snorts of warning or alarm and watches its would-be attacker.

If a lion can get to within about twenty or thirty yards of a prey animal without being detected, it is likely to rush at high speed and try to catch it. It may or may not be successful, and usually is not. The intended victim may be too alert, too swift, or too nimble at avoiding the lion; or, on the other hand, it may stumble, collide with another prey animal, or choose a poor escape route. Only about one in five of these chases ends in success – from the lion's point of view. The decision by a stalking lioness whether to charge at once or whether to try to get closer and so improve the chances of success must be an extremely difficult one, influenced by many, largely unpredictable, factors. She has to weigh up whether the prey animals are likely to move away spontaneously, or whether they might wander nearer; whether they are likely to detect any further approach by her; how they might behave

52 A lioness walking across open country is 'escorted' by observant Thomson's gazelles, which run across her path. A visible lion in open country is no threat to a healthy ungulate

when she sprints; whether there are any particularly vulnerable prey animals present on whom to concentrate; and what her chances are of another attempt later. In the course of lions' evolution, some compromise balance between all these factors has clearly been reached. This compromise is not expressed in a simple form such as that it is worth rushing if prey are within, say, twenty yards. The distance depends on the circumstances. I have seen an experienced adult lioness rush successfully from as far away as fifty yards, and have seen another desist for some time from rushing from a distance of ten yards at a passing line of zebras until a foal came past.

There are a number of ways in which lions can improve their chances of success. The first is by hunting at night, as Schaller showed, and most hunting does in fact occur in the two hours after dark and then in the four hours before dawn. Lions can see much better at night than we can. There is a reflecting layer behind the retina in a cat's eye which, in effect, enables the light to be used twice, so making the eye more sensitive at very low light levels. A sign of this was when in the dark I caught a lion's eyes in the beam of a spotlight: they would shine very brightly for a moment until the lion blinked or looked away. However, most ungulates also have better night vision than we have, and their eyes also reflect. When I was driving at night with lights the first indication of the presence of a herd of animals was usually the sight of a cluster of bright spots in the distance, and the way in which these eyes flickered and moved often betrayed their species before I could see their bodies. The advantage to lions of hunting at night rather than by day probably lies not in their superior vision at night, but in the fact that for all animals, lions and prey alike, the visibility is poorer, the shadows deeper and the cover more concealing. However, a lion cannot necessarily do all its hunting at night, for the opportunities may simply not arise. Some, for example, occur only during the day: gazelles only come to drink at the water-holes where they are vulnerable in the daytime, and warthogs are only active by day.

The other main way in which lions can improve their success rate in hunting is by doing so communally, and this is their commonest method. When prey have been detected, a wildebeest herd perhaps, the lions start to stalk towards them. As they get close, they take different routes, some going on straight ahead and some to the sides, so the prey herd is approached by lions stalking towards them from different directions. This is a fairly primitive form of co-operation, in that all the lions are stalking independently, yet they watch one another, and clearly pay attention to where their companions are and what they are doing. Eventually one lion gets close enough to make a rush at a wildebeest, or else a lion is detected by the prey. In either case the wildebeest all start running, chased by one or more lions. In the course of the confusion it often happens that a prey animal fleeing from one lion runs within range of another whom it has not seen, and who sprints and catches it. Hunts like this are about twice as likely to be successful as solitary hunts: perhaps one in three ends with a kill. Some end with two or sometimes more kills, as more than one hunter manages to catch a wildebeest which ran too close to it. Wildebeest seem to be particularly vulnerable in this respect: on a number of occasions I found multiple kills of this species, but rarely of others.

One curious and striking feature of lions' markings – the black backs of their ears – must help them in their communal hunting. A lion head in the grass in front of you is much more noticeable if it is looking away than if it is looking at you, because these black marks are very distinctive from behind. No doubt they have evolved partly because they help lions to keep track of one another, which would be useful both for cubs learning to hunt and for adults hunting communally. They were certainly useful for me when looking for hunting lions. From in front, however, the direction in which prey would be looking, these distinctive marks are invisible.

Large cubs and subadult lions may also take part in these communal hunts, and presumably by their participation they gain experience in the process of catching prey. It is difficult to know how much these youngsters actually help by their participation. I have seen many stalks which failed because a young lion stood up or moved at the wrong time; on the other hand, the more hunters there are, even relatively inefficient ones, the more difficult it must be for a prey animal to know which way to run to escape.

Some of the early explorers' and hunters' descriptions of lions hunting included reports of a remarkable degree of co-operation. One of the best-known statements is that some lions stampede prey towards other lions waiting to ambush them; sometimes they are reported to do this by roaring, sometimes by letting the prey detect their scent and sometimes by driving them openly. I cannot deny that such hunts may occur, but I do question the interpretation of what was seen, particularly if it imputed very elaborate and deliberate co-operation. In the Serengeti, at least, I never heard lions roar when hunting. Another lion who is nearby but not hunting may well happen to roar at an opportune

53 Watched by a couple of cubs, three lionesses set off to stalk towards possible prey. Note the conspicuous black backs of their ears, which help lions to keep in contact when hunting co-operatively. The lioness on the right has lost her tail, as described at the end of Chapter 11

moment, especially if he is male. But I never saw prey animals really pay any attention to lions roaring, perhaps precisely because it means that the latter are not in fact hunting; and certainly they do not stampede in a panic. I do not think that such tactics would work, anyway, for prey which have become alerted to the presence of a nearby predator generally move away from cover where there might be lurking attackers, and so are likely to be *more* difficult to catch, rather than less.

In the Serengeti, too, lions do not appear to have learnt the importance of wind direction. Schaller showed that they are as likely to go down wind towards their prey as up, in spite of the fact that their downwind approaches were much less likely to be successful because the prey detected their scent. If they fail to take into account this point, which is in fact a complicated one for them to learn, they are unlikely to use it in an elaborate ambushing strategy. On the other hand lions are intelligent and adaptable animals, and they may well use strategies in some areas which they have not developed in others. But I think it is fair to say that the more elaborate hunting strategies which have been reported are not common and have not been properly investigated.

The hunts I have described may take place anywhere. There are no such things as 'hunting grounds' as far as lions are concerned – lions hunt their prey wherever those prey are and where they can be caught. Hunts tend to be more successful where the cover is thicker, at drinking places, and at points where prey animals cross rivers. On the other hand, prey animals tend not to linger at such dangerous places, so lions must often hunt elsewhere where the circumstances are less advantageous for them. Knowledge of their territory certainly helps. A lion may run to a waterhole where it knows there may be prey animals drinking, although it cannot see them. I watched a group of lions running fast and quite openly at a wildebeest herd which they knew could become trapped in a loop in a river with no crossing point; it was the right strategy to use in the circumstances, and it proved successful in providing them with a gnu dinner.

It is difficult to define when lions are looking for prey. Once they have seen it, they may be said to be hunting when they orientate or advance towards it in a crouched or stalking posture. But much more of their time is spent not orientating or advancing towards prey, although they would do so if prey were to appear. Should they be said to be hunting at these times? When waiting inactive they are alert, and if a suitable opportunity arises they will start to hunt. Similarly, when moving around in their area they will hunt prey if they come across it, but it is difficult to tell how much they are moving actually in search of prey. The groups of lions which I was radio-tracking tended to move relatively short distances for the first night or two after they had made and eaten a kill but, although fairly full, they quite often caught another animal during these nights. If they did not, and so had gone for several days without food, they appeared to change their food-getting strategy. They then moved over much larger distances each night, and the likelihood of catching prey went up. Thus one may say that the lion's food-procuring method is to a fairly large extent an opportunistic one, at any rate under favourable circumstances.

This opportunism shows itself, too, in other methods of hunting. Although perhaps nine out of ten hunts are of the type I have described, a proportion of lions' prey is caught by other methods. Lions may come across a very sick or wounded prey animal which they simply run and catch. They may come across an animal asleep. Sometimes they flush a young antelope, whose newborn young protect themselves by remaining concealed and motionless until almost trodden upon; in that case the lions usually chase and frequently catch it.

Most chases are short. The lion sprints, and if it does not catch its prey within a relatively few yards, is outdistanced by it and gives up. However, a few animals can be run down by lions, particularly warthog piglets and gazelle fawns. The lions may start running after these from a considerable distance away, and catch them after a chase of two or three hundred yards. I have also seen a lioness running down in this way a gazelle with a broken leg, but it took a surprisingly long chase to do so.

Another way of catching a particular type of prey – warthogs – is by digging them out of their burrows. This is an arduous and time-consuming task which, in my study area, the lions indulged in only when they were very short of food and when the ground was relatively soft in the wet season. The digging consists of removing the roof of the tunnel, thus forming a long and deepening trench. Even an adult lioness could probably crawl down at least some warthog holes; indeed I once saw two almost full-grown subadults completely disappear underground down the hole of a warthog which had just run out from that hole. A lioness does not normally do so; she is probably deterred by

54 A warthog kneeling as he grazes

the warthog's long sharp pointed tusks which would slash and injure her badly in the narrow confines of the tunnel were she to try. But once the tunnel has been excavated, the warthog can be pulled out or grabbed from above.

These various methods of getting food all refer to catching prey, but lions also get a proportion of their food by scavenging: in other words the prey was dead before the lion came across it. A large number of animals die of natural causes, and if a lion finds one of these, naturally it feeds upon it. As well as being catholic feeders lions will, if hungry, eat food which is extremely old and decomposed. Such carcasses they may find by smell, if the carcass is in thick cover, but often the carcass is out in the open and is detected first by the most efficient scavengers, the vultures. These have a high vantage point as they soar across the sky, and they can cover large distances effortlessly. When a vulture spots a dead animal it glides steeply down in a straight line to the food source, the air singing through its wing feathers. Soaring vultures watch one another, and on seeing one of their number descend they plummet down to the food too. Lions and hyaenas are among the scavengers which also keep an eye on vultures, and on seeing several come down will often head in that direction and obtain a meal themselves from the carcass which the birds have found. Hyaenas, being more mobile animals, often get there before lions do, but lions being larger can almost always oust them.

Lions may also rob hyaenas of kills which the latter have made. Hans Kruuk showed that hyaenas are not, in fact, pure scavengers any more than lions are pure predators, and they often hunt in packs at night and kill prey animals themselves. A pack disposes of its kill quickly amid a great deal of squabbling and the famous hyaena giggling 'laughter'. Lions are often attracted to the sound of hyaenas on a kill, and can even be lured to a spot by playing tape-recordings of this cacophony. If they arrive in time they can usually dispossess the hyaenas and feed on what remains of their prey. Lions rob the other large cats too, and in the next two chapters I describe how they obtain food from leopards and cheetahs. One night I came across a male lion about twenty feet up a tree trying, unsuccessfully, to reach the dikdik kill of a leopard in the too slender branches several feet higher up; subsequently he had great difficulty in coming down the tree trunk backwards, and certainly he did not benefit from this attempt at scavenging. Other providers of dead meat such as wild dogs or jackals are also robbed by lions if the opportunity arises, although it seldom does.

The distinction between predation and scavenging is a blurred one. The term predation usually indicates capturing and killing live prey, while scavenging indicates the procuring of dead prey. But is it predation or scavenging when a lion feeds on a buffalo which is lying dying of disease? Or when lions rob a leopard of an impala which it has not yet killed? Or when a lion eats some partly incubated ostrich eggs? All these instances, which I have known to occur, obscure the somewhat arbitrary division of food-getting into predation or scavenging. On the whole scavenging provides perhaps one-seventh of a lion's food.

In addition to scavenging from other species, lions also scavenge from one another. After a successful communal hunt most lions, and of course all the cubs, are feeding on prey which was captured by only one of their number. Males, however, take the process a stage further. A resident pride male does relatively little hunting. If he is with a group of females who are hunting, the male takes little part, tending to follow along in a rather inactive way until the females have been successful. Alternatively he may come across females with a kill in the course of his movements around his territory. In either case a male lion, being half as large again as a female, is able to muscle in on the kill and feed from it. Often he takes over almost the whole carcass: the phrase 'the lion's share' refers to the male lion and has a basis in biological fact, as I saw many times. Almost all the food caught by lions is caught by the females, who thus provide food not only for their dependent cubs but also for partially food-parasitic males. The males are not incapable of hunting – indeed they are quick off the mark to take advantage of an unexpected opportunity if one should arise – but usually they do not seem to bother, and it may be that they are less good at hunting than the females. It is possible that their bulk makes them slower, or that their size and mane hinder their stalking. On the other hand their size may help them to tackle large prey, such as a bull buffalo, which few prides in my area went in for. Young males who have left their natal pride and not yet found a pride which they can take over have to find their own food. Although scavenged food forms a larger proportion of their diet at this stage, they also hunt effectively for themselves. They have to learn to do so, and there are many reports of young males being injured and killed by the buffaloes which they themselves were trying to kill.

55 A bull buffalo in the prime of life, chewing a mouthful of grass. Their size, and their massive horns, protect healthy adult buffaloes from extensive predation by lions

56 A lioness kills a wildebeest by holding its throat until it falls

If a hunt is successful, a lioness catches up with and brings down a prey animal. She does this, not by leaping onto the animal's back as is often supposed, but actually by seizing the rump or shoulders with her claws; the prey is almost always fleeing fast at this stage so is thrown off balance and falls to the ground. The lioness then quickly bites and holds it by either the throat or the muzzle, thus preventing it from getting to its feet again and keeping herself clear of flailing hooves or horns.

I examined many lion kills to see how they had been killed; in very few was the neck broken, and in those cases the break could well have been caused after death. Clearly lions in the Serengeti do not generally kill their victims by breaking their necks as pumas, for example, are reported to do. A prey animal held down by a lion at its throat or nose dies within a few minutes from a combination of strangulation, suffocation, shock and loss of blood if, as often happens, other members of the pride have already started feeding from its other end. Thus lions do not kill particularly swiftly or painlessly – presumably there has not been selective pressure on them to do so, nor on prey animals to die quickly. Small prey animals, such as impalas or gazelles, may be killed much more quickly by being bitten in the neck and then torn apart by several lions struggling at the carcass. Lions rarely play with their prey before killing it as domestic cats do. Most of their victims are too large for this to be a wise thing for the lion to try, for they might then defend themselves. The only exception I saw was when adult lionesses who had captured a subadult eland did not kill it but withdrew a few yards and watched their two-year-old cubs slowly manage to do so.

Feeding usually starts at the groin where the skin is soft. The skin is partly cut by the carnassial teeth and partly pulled or torn open along the belly. The viscera are dragged out. The intestines are usually eaten first, the lion drawing them in through its incisor teeth and squeezing out their contents; they probably contain a high proportion of vitamins and fat. The stomach often gets pulled a few yards away, and then or later a lion often rakes pieces of grass, sticks and dirt over it, for no obviously important reason.

How much of the carcass is eaten, and how quickly, depends on how big it is, on the number of lions feeding at it, and on how hungry they are. The flesh is eaten from the femurs first, and then the skin pulled back so that the feeders can get at the meat on the back of the forelimbs.

The skin is not usually consumed although it may be if the lions are short of food, but it is pulled off the skeleton. The limbs are dislocated at the pelvis and shoulders, and the skull is often separated from the vertebral column. All are cleaned of blood and flesh by a combination of licking, pulling with the canines and cutting with the carnassials. Cleaned bones remain marking the site of a lion kill. Hyaenas and jackals may carry bones away, so missing limbs indicated that one of these other scavengers had been at the kill. Those species carry off pieces of a kill either to eat elsewhere or to take to their offspring; lions very rarely do either.

The kill, or pieces of it, may be moved short distances. A lion often drags an entire carcass into the shade or into cover. The kill is held by the neck and pulled by the lion moving backwards with very heavy carcasses or, if possible, forwards with the carcass between the forelegs. Kills may be dragged up to about a hundred yards to a more suitable site. If some meat remains on the carcass but the lion or lions are full, they usually guard it and feed again several hours later. The presence of a lion beside a kill keeps hyaenas, jackals and particularly vultures away from it; without such guarding kills would rarely provide lions with a second meal.

An adult lioness needs of the order of 12 lb of meat per day; males need more, and cubs less. This quantity is not taken in regularly: usually a much larger amount is eaten when a kill is made, followed by days of scarcity. An empty lioness can consume four or five days' worth of meat during one feed lasting a few hours. With 60 lb of meat inside her she has a swollen belly and appears to be uncomfortable. Males can take in more, up to about 90 lb. However, if there are a number of lions in the group, most of them do not manage to take in such quantities from a single kill.

How often lions feed is partly a matter of chance, but depends also on the size of the prey, its abundance and the number of lions in the group hunting together. When they are feeding on relatively large prey animals such as zebra or wildebeest, a small group feeds on average at three-day intervals. A large pride, with many well-grown cubs, probably feeds most nights, each animal taking in less. So do they at times when very large numbers of migratory prey animals are in their area; then they manage to make more kills than they need, leaving some of them largely uneaten. This may happen, too, when a hunting group makes a large multiple killing. The largest such killing I found consisted of nine wildebeest slaughtered; they had been surprised while a

130

57 A lioness chews at a carcass, cutting at the skin with her shearing cheek teeth. Her flanks are festooned with flies

58 A lioness drags her wildebeest victim towards cover and shade, where she can feed in privacy and be cooler

59 In a thicket, two lionesses and three cubs feed together at the remains of a wildebeest

herd was crossing a steep-sided river valley, and killed as they struggled helplessly out of it. Only two of the victims were eaten: the rest were left almost untouched by the lions and were totally consumed by vultures. When lions are hungry and feeding on small prey such as impalas or gazelles, they take in a much higher proportion of the carcass: they eat the skin and chew at the smaller bones, cracking and swallowing small pieces of them which later reappear in their droppings. Lions probably consume, on average, about two-thirds to three-quarters of a prey animal they kill; the remainder is skeleton, skin and wastage. On the other hand, a proportion of their food is scavenged. Therefore, on average, a total of a little over two tons of prey is killed per year to feed each adult lioness. This corresponds to about ten adult zebra mares, or sixteen wildebeest cows, or forty impala males. However, since a proportion of the prey killed are younger, smaller animals, the numbers taken are proportionately larger.

Lions are recorded as having eaten almost every animal from aardvarks to zebras, including porcupines and people, lion cubs, elephants, hares, hippos and hyaenas. A list of species which somewhere sometime have been killed by lions would be an enormously long one and rather unhelpful in describing lions' normal diet. A list of the relative numbers of different species taken is of more interest. However, any such list is liable to contain considerable biases, depending upon how the information is collected. I was not watching lions continuously, even if it had been possible to do, because this would have disturbed and distorted their hunting. I observed them at intervals, and naturally I could see them better during the day than at night, so I was more likely to observe predation on a small diurnal species in the daytime then on a small nocturnal one. Another bias arises because a lion will remain for at least a couple of days near a buffalo kill, while it takes less than an hour for it to consume all traces of a gazelle fawn; therefore I or anyone else would be much less likely to find gazelle kills and might therefore think that gazelles were killed more rarely than is really the case. We must bear in mind such biases, and the way in which kill data have been gathered, when considering lists of lion kills.

Several factors determine which species occur in a particular lion pride's diet in the course of a year, and in what proportions. The first, obviously, is which prey species inhabit the pride's territory. However, some of these prey species are migratory and are within the lions' area for only part of the year: obviously lions cannot kill wildebeest when there are no wildebeest anywhere near them. When both zebras and wildebeest are present in a pride's area in the Serengeti more of the latter tend to be killed by lions – I think they are easier to catch – but over the whole park and over the whole year more zebras are killed than wildebeest. Zebras are more widely dispersed and are to be found in more prides' areas and for a greater proportion of each year.

Another factor influencing what lions eat is the numbers of each prey species among the population from which those lions are taking their toll. In general, the commoner the species, the more of that species are killed, simply because the chances that lions will encounter one of them are higher. A lion does not just take its pick from an array of potential prey; it spends a considerable amount of time in searching for a prey animal to start to hunt, at which it will then probably be unsuccessful. This problem in finding prey may seem surprising to anyone who has seen photographs of the Serengeti or other parks, apparently teeming with wildlife. It is worth remembering, though, that people tend to take photographs where the animals are, rather than of all the other empty spaces where they are not. The total weight of all prey animals in the whole Serengeti ecosystem divided by the total area comes to an average of only about 120 wildebeest-sized animals per square mile. Since a large proportion of the prey usually live in big herds, there are naturally a great many empty spaces elsewhere which are devoid of animals for lions to hunt. I sometimes drove for miles without seeing any lion food. As well as its numbers, the distribution of the prey species over the area naturally influences the chances that a lion will encounter one of that species. A lion is less likely to come across a wildebeest if these live in dense herds than if the same number of them were scattered more evenly all over the countryside.

The size and habits of the prey, what defences it has against predators and its catchability all influence how many are taken by lions. Elephants, rhinoceroses and hippopotami are all too large and well armed to be taken regularly by lions, although young or very sick individuals are occasionally preyed upon. Buffaloes and giraffes are both almost too large; adults of these species can rarely be taken by single lions, but are often killed by lions hunting co-operatively, and many of their young are also killed by lions. The commonest lion food is from this size downwards – zebra, wildebeest, hartebeest, topi, eland, waterbuck, impala, gazelle and warthog. These are not powerful enough to defend themselves against lions, and they almost invariably flee rather than make any attempt to do so. Their main way of avoiding ending up inside a lion is to be thoroughly alert, and where possible to avoid places where a lion might be concealed. But a prey animal cannot spend all its time looking round for predators if it is to get enough food itself; it cannot avoid going to danger points such as waterholes if it is not to die of dehydration; and it cannot be forever running from the slightest suspicious sound or scent if it is not to wear itself out. So a

60 Wildebeest move over the skyline

compromise has been reached in the course of the prey's evolution, a compromise between excessive caution and carelessness.

A wide variety of small animals are very occasionally killed by lions – dikdiks, hyraxes, hares, jackals, small rodents, vervet monkeys and guinea fowl. These are rarely hunted in an organized way, but are seized if the opportunity presents itself. Clearly the amount of food obtained from prey as small as a dikdik is tiny. Yet lions will expend considerable energy in running down gazelle fawns, which must provide equally little edible return, so it is presumably worth the lions' while if they can catch them. Thus it is likely that an important reason for not hunting many small prey animals is that such hunts would be most unlikely to suceed. Among the thicker vegetation where such small prey species generally live, a small animal can probably dodge and escape from a much larger predator with little difficulty. Lions' size enables them to take large prey, and by the same token makes it more difficult for them to catch small prey.

There is no evidence that lions 'prefer' to eat one species as compared with another, although it is quite possible that they do. Different kinds of meat taste different, and lions do avoid eating some kinds of otherwise fresh meat – such as a newly killed hyaena, and in some places waterbuck – when they will feed on very rotten buffalo meat, for example. Certainly some prey species are killed more often than their abundance would lead one to expect if lions were catching prey at random, or on the basis of relative abundance. In Nairobi National Park, for example, wildebeest have for years formed a greater proportion of lion meals than of the live prey population. Judith Rudnai showed that this species contributed a quarter of the Nairobi lion kills although only about one in fourteen of the live prey were wildebeest. This does not necessarily mean that lions prefer the taste of wildebeest meat, or indeed that they make any extra effort to catch wildebeest. It may be simply that they encounter wildebeest more often or that wildebeest are less successful at escaping. Lions doubtless learn from

61 a&b Two less important prey species of lions – two elands browsing and a hartebeest resting

their successes and failures, and will continue to hunt in places and
using methods which have proved successful in the past. I found what
looked like specialization in different prides: for example, one of the
prides I studied took buffaloes much more often than other prides did,
possibly because the lions in that pride had learnt a specialized technique for dealing with these powerful and dangerous animals. On the
other hand it is possible that some features of their territory or of the
behaviour of the buffaloes there made the latter particularly vulnerable. In places such as the Kalahari region, lions prey to a considerable
extent upon porcupines, which is apparently a very hazardous pursuit,
especially for young lions who have not yet learnt whatever is the
correct technique for dealing with them. One lion's meat is another
lion's prickly problem. In the Serengeti, where porcupines are enormously outnumbered by other prey species, lions usually take little notice
of them. I have even seen a couple of porcupines sniffing and chewing at
the remains of a kill while the lions were still there themselves; the latter
were interested in the porcupines but made no attempt to molest them.
  The numbers of each species killed by lions does not, then, bear a

simple relationship to their numbers in the environment. Nor does it within each species as regards numbers of the different age or sex categories, because these are vulnerable in different ways. A greater proportion of very young animals are taken from most prey species than would be expected on the basis of their relative numbers in the live population; this is not surprising, because newborn animals cannot run as fast as adults, and there may also be among them a higher proportion of defective or inferior individuals not yet weeded out by natural selection, operating partly through predation. It is likely, too, that the relative conspicuousness of young animals also helps to render them more vulnerable. For example, when a drinking zebra herd stampedes in panic away from a river on being ambushed by lions, picking out one individual from the rushing throng of dazzling black and white rumps and flanks must present a problem to the sprinting lion. A zebra much smaller than its companions would provide a target on which to focus and at which to aim.

In general old animals are caught relatively often too. With their teeth wearing down, making feeding less efficient, with the cumulative effects of disease and accidents, and with the other physiological results

62 A family group of zebras – a stallion with his mares and foals. Zebras provide more lion food in the Serengeti than any other species

63 Two male impalas clash in a territorial dispute. Such fighting makes males particularly vulnerable to predation – it is conspicuous, exhausting and takes up all the attention of the combatants

138

of ageing, old animals tend to be slower both to react and to run, and thus are more likely to be caught by lions. Disease and other factors such as stress which contribute to poor condition also make some animals more vulnerable than others.

The males of many prey species bear a heavier load of lion predation than do the females. There are several reasons for this. The first is their distribution: most ungulates have a form of harem or territorial system as a result of which the males tend to be scattered and spaced out while the females are in groups with only one male. Thus a hunting lion is much more likely to encounter a male hartebeest, for example, than a group containing females, and I noticed the same effect myself when travelling in my study area. Second, single prey animals, which tend to be the males, are more vulnerable than those in groups, probably because several pairs of eyes, ears and nostrils are better than one at detecting the approach of a predator. George Schaller showed that lions were more likely to be successful when hunting single prey individuals than when hunting prey which were in groups. Third, as a result of the strenuous competition among males for females or for territories, male ungulates often tend to wear themselves out and thus be in poorer condition and so more vulnerable than their females. Each year at the end of the very energetic wildebeest rutting season I used to come across a large number of completely exhausted males who had spent perhaps a month in almost non-stop running – herding females, fighting with rival males – and had had scarcely any spare time in which to feed. Such worn-out animals are easily caught by lions. Fourth, their fighting and displaying makes them incautious, and is often so noisy and conspicuous that it attracts the attention of a predator. Fifth, expelled males may have to occupy inferior areas which expose them more to predation, such as more thickly wooded country. Finally, they are often more conspicuous. When selecting one individual from a group it is possible that the rushing lion may select and fixate on the one animal which stands out from the others because of its size or horns, and this would mean the male. Against these factors contributing to higher male mortality at the teeth of lions must be set the increased vulnerability of females which are pregnant or giving birth. Nonetheless, in general more males are killed than females, up to twice as many in some species. In others, such as zebras which stay in cohesive family groups containing both sexes, there is little differential predation between the sexes.

I do not wish to give the impression that lions only catch young, old, sick or weak victims, because they do not. Most of their prey are healthy subadult or adult animals, as far as I could tell from examining many of their kills; so are most of the live prey populations from which those victims were taken, as far as I could tell from external appearances. Nevertheless, there was a higher proportion of those especially vulnerable categories among animals killed by lions than among those not killed. All are to some extent vulnerable. Chance probably plays a large part in deciding *which* zebra happens to wander close to a hidden lion, *which* occupied warthog burrow happens to lie in the path of a hungry lion pride, or *which* wildebeest happens to have its head down having a meal when a lioness rushes at a herd to claim hers.

7 · The leopard

To help understand both the uniqueness and the elaborate nature of the lion social system, it is worth taking a brief look at the two other large cats which occupy the same environment, the leopard and in the next chapter, the cheetah.

I want to consider the leopard from two different angles. First, the lion and leopard live in many of the same habitats; they both feed on other mammals and so to some extent are ecological competitors. Both are adapted to their environment but in different ways: they have taken different ecological routes. The lion's niche is that of the large, group-hunting cat, while the leopard's is that of a solitary, unspecialized and therefore adaptable cat. Second, we can reasonably look on the leopard as similar to the lion prototype. Almost all the other cat species in the world are solitary, and where anything is known of their social organization it appears to resemble that of the leopard. The joint ancestor of the lion and leopard before they diverged was probably similar in structure, social organization and behaviour to the present-day leopard. During this discussion of the leopard it is worth bearing in mind that this is probably what lions were like before they started out along their particular specialization of social hunting and living.

Most leopards are timid: they remain concealed in thick cover and flee if they are detected. While studying lions I made notes on any leopards I came across, and built up a photographic file of each individual who allowed me to approach close enough to photograph it. I also managed to put radio-collars onto three leopards. It took considerable time to find animals who would even once let me get close enough to dart them in order to collar them. When they were wearing radio-collars, for several months I could find these individuals

64 A young female leopard, just immobilized. She has a dart in her shoulder, and a radio-collar round her neck which I am about to remove. She still has her swallowing and chewing reflexes, and is licking her lips

65 A young male leopard, still with pink muzzle and perfect ears, peers at me through the flowering grass heads

whenever I wanted. They rapidly became accustomed to my presence and as a result I could observe them from close range without disturbing their behaviour.

Leopards are much smaller than lions, being only about one-third of the weight of the latter and, as in lions, males are much bigger than females. Of the few animals which I managed to weigh, adult females were around 75 lb and males around 130 lb, but there is no way of knowing how typical these weights are. As expected of such an adaptable species, leopards from different regions may be of very different sizes; desert ones, for example, are probably smaller than forest ones, but there is little reliable information to go on. Hunters who have shot leopards for trophies tend if they can to choose large ones, they rarely weigh their victims, and they are apt to publicize the sizes only of particularly large animals; thus it is exceedingly difficult to determine average weights.

It is well known that leopards are covered in black spots; these are arranged in rings or rosettes on the yellowish fur over most of the body but at the extremities (the head, feet, and tail), the rosettes break down. I used the arrangement of spots on the head to recognize different individuals. Every leopard, it turns out, has a different pattern of spots on its face and around its eyes. The same is probably true of the whole body, but elsewhere the skin stretches according to the animal's posture and there are no good reference points, such as the eye, to use for comparing spot-patterns. Other advantages of using the head spots are that these are more likely to be what leopards themselves use and so to differ more between individuals, that the head is often the only part of the leopard which can be seen, and that when other people photograph leopards they naturally try to include the face. As a result I have been able to use photographs taken by other people to identify individual leopards. Most good photographs of leopards in the wild are taken in the Serengeti, and I have often been able to recognize the animals shown in postcards, magazine articles, and airline or safari firm advertisements. One can even see sometimes that the photograph has been printed the wrong way round, because the spots on the two sides of the face are different! From my photographs and other pictures it has been possible to build up records of a few Serengeti leopards stretching back for quite a number of years: fortunately leopards don't change their spots.

Leopards vary in colour, some being considerably darker than others. Melanistic individuals occur which are black all over, with the spots often still visible as even darker black marks. These black animals tend particularly to inhabit thick forest and high altitude regions, where a black coat is presumably as effective a camouflage as a normal one. In more open country a motionless spotted leopard is difficult to detect, for its spots help to break up its outline and its colour scheme does not contrast with its background.

This variability of leopards has for years caused confusion in their nomenclature. The Roman name *leopardus* reflects this confusion and the belief that the leopard was a hybrid of a lion (*leo*) and a 'pard' or panther. Nowadays the term panther has no precise meaning. It is used (though better forgotten, I think) to refer to leopards, jaguars and other such large cats, and particularly to the black varieties of these species. More recently the great variation in size and markings between leopards from different parts of its large range has caused the species *Panthera pardus* to be subdivided by taxonomists into a number of different races.

Leopards have relatively longer tails than lions, and they lack the tail tuft at the end; instead the tip of the leopard's tail is white on the

66 A leopard stands on a kopje, showing its elegant shape

underside. When its owner walks normally this white patch is scarcely visible, but when a leopard is apparently wanting to be conspicuous, such as when she is being followed by cubs, she walks with her tail held in a high curve upwards and then the end of it acts as a highly visible flag. Black leopards obviously cannot display this signal, and no one knows whether or how they compensate for their inability to do so.

Compared with lions, too, the neck is thicker relative to the size of the head. This was graphically demonstrated for me by an adult female leopard which I darted and fitted with a radio-collar. The collar must have been just too large because by the next morning she had got it off, and her collared cub was carrying it around as though needing a spare! A week later I put the same collar onto the same female leopard again, this time reducing its size by only half an inch; it was then definitely just on the tight side.

RANGE AND HABITAT

In keeping with its adaptability, the leopard has a larger geographical range than any of the other large cat species. Despite an enormous reduction in numbers in the last half century, the species is still distributed almost throughout Africa, stretching east across the Middle East, India and the mainland of south-east Asia, and north through eastern China to Manchuria. Over this vast area it occupies a wide variety of different types of habitats too. Leopards are found (or rather they *live*, because they are actually extremely difficult to find!) in habitats ranging from semi-desert to rain forest, being particularly abundant in the latter. In thick forest, though, they are exceedingly difficult to study and almost nothing is known about them there. They live near sea level and up to surprisingly high altitudes; one has even been found frozen in the snow near the summit of Mount Kilimanjaro, at 19,000 feet the highest mountain in Africa.

Climatic conditions, therefore, seem to be relatively unimportant to leopards; to survive in an area they seem to require only a population of prey animals and sufficient cover in which to hide and catch those prey. They were fairly common in my woodland study area in the Serengeti, and although I saw them nowhere nearly as often I would guess that there were between a third and a half as many of them as there were lions. Leopards do not inhabit the completely open, treeless plains but they do exist along the sparsely vegetated stream beds which meander off from the plains, and in the rock outcrops which are scattered here and there on the otherwise bare, flat landscape. On the whole, where there are trees and rocks there will be leopards, unless man has managed to remove them.

The key to the leopard's success lies in its hunting methods. The leopard is a solitary stalker. When it has seen a potential prey animal, it moves stealthily and silently towards it. It is even better than a lion at using any cover there may be, and in a leopard's habitat there is likely to be more vegetation to hide him than there is concealment for a hunting lioness in hers. Also leopards, being much smaller than lions, need less cover to remain invisible and are better camouflaged. The body of a stalking leopard, gliding through the vegetation, over obstacles and down hollows, looks almost snakelike – if you see it. If the prey animal looks up alert, the leopard is instantly motionless, remaining so until the potential victim relaxes. One leopard I was watching took nearly three-quarters of an hour over an unsuccessful eighty-yard stalk towards a resting duiker. When close enough, which usually means very close, the leopard dashes suddenly and fast; if it is lucky it seizes or pulls down the prey with its claws, and immediately bites its victim.

However, adept stalker though it is, the leopard nonetheless usually fails with its hunt because its intended prey animals are too alert. It is very difficult for a leopard to move close to its intended victim without giving any indication at all of its presence, and if the prey detects any suspicious movement or smell it can usually escape if it flees at once. Birds can fly off and thus escape into the third dimension; rodents and hyraxes can slip into crevices or holes too deep for leopards' claws; hares and dikdiks can dodge round bushes and other obstacles more nimbly than a large leopard; and gazelles and impalas do not need much of a start to be able to outdistance a leopard. These were some of the reasons why only three out of the sixty-four hunting attempts I actually witnessed by my closely observed leopards were successful. Admittedly most of the attempts I watched took place in daylight, because it was only then that I could observe them without disturbing the process, and it is likely that at night their success rate is somewhat higher. Nonetheless, as with lions, it is clear from my observations that most hunts by leopards also fail.

Sometimes they fail for the same reason as with lions – that the hunter pays no attention to the wind direction, thus allowing its

67 A leopard carries an impala fawn. Note the different kinds of spots on different parts of her body – rosettes on the back and flanks, large spots on the lower limbs, small spots on the head and a necklace below the neck

intended prey to catch its scent and move quickly out of danger. I once watched and filmed an experienced adult female leopard stalking cross-wind towards a resting gazelle through patchy long grass. When she came to a bare area she obviously had to go either left or right to get within the last few necessary yards of the gazelle. In both directions there was cover which would have concealed her but, despite my willing her not to, she went left, which was upwind. The rest was predictable: the gazelle suddenly sprang to its feet with a snort of alarm, stood tense and alert for a moment and then ran quickly and jerkily downwind. He probably never saw the leopard until she rose and walked openly back to the tree from which she had noticed him. An animal can easily learn that smells come from upwind, but it is much more difficult for it to learn that it has a smell itself, which travels downwind. In other places both lions and leopards may learn the importance of wind direction when stalking, although this has not yet been demonstrated convincingly, but obviously in the Serengeti many manage to survive successfully without doing so.

Leopards are opportunistic hunters. If a chance presents itself, they take it at once. A leopard up a tree lying half asleep on a branch will come down and stalk a prey animal if it sees one which looks vulnerable. There are no regular hunting places or times. Probably most hunting occurs at night and, particularly if leopards are persecuted by humans, they become almost totally nocturnal. In the Serengeti, though, they may be active and hunting for a couple of hours after dawn, and also when the temperature drops just before dusk. Leopards are more nocturnal than lions, but not much more.

In their adaptable way, leopards use other methods of hunting apart from the stalking I have described. They may ambush prey animals, waiting motionless until a victim happens to come near; there are many reports of leopards concealing themselves close to tracks where prey animals are accustomed to pass. Although there are numerous unsubstantiated accounts of leopards dropping off branches on to passing antelopes, such behaviour does not occur commonly, if at all, in the Serengeti. The relatively open country there would make it a most unprofitable means of procuring food, and I remain unconvinced that it would be effective elsewhere either.

My radio-collared young female leopard used to go openly from clump to clump of grass, investigating each to see whether any possible victim was concealed there. Sometimes she would flush a dikdik in this way, or more often a hare, and would dash after the zig-zagging, fleeing animal, just occasionally managing to catch it. She had another method for hunting rock hyraxes, rushing onto and over an apparently deserted rock kopje and chasing after the startled scattering hyraxes as they scampered to the safety of their crevices.

Leopards, like lions, obtain some of their food by scavenging from carcasses which died from other causes. My radio-collared animals scavenged meals from the carcasses of giraffes, buffaloes, zebras and kongonis. One also obtained a small piece of meat dropped by an eagle flying low over her. She took a surprisingly long time to find it by smell; had she had useful colour vision like me, she would have been able at once to pick out the bright red meat amid the short green grass.

Having caught and killed her prey, the leopard usually takes it to cover before starting to feed on it. Often, if the kill is large, the leopard carries it up a tree, behaviour which perhaps explains her powerful thick neck. It is a most spectacular sight to see a leopard hold in her mouth an animal almost as large as herself and climb up a tree as though it weighed almost nothing: leopards have prodigious strength for their size, for they certainly carry rather than drag their load up into the branches. They experience more difficulty in carrying the prey *down*, if they decide to move it to a different tree, as they did once or

148

68 Contrast in coat patterns – a young male leopard scavenges a meal from the end of a giraffe which has died of natural causes

69 A leopard carries an adult gazelle up a tree. She has prodigious strength, for the gazelle weighs two-thirds as much as she does

twice before they had become accustomed to the presence of my car close to them. Their claws point in the wrong direction for coming down and the swinging body of the prey makes balancing more awkward. They do not seem to have hit on the idea of just dropping the carcass and collecting it at the bottom!

Once a carcass is lodged in the branches of a tree it is safe from hyaenas and usually from lions. With many of these competing predator-scavengers around, such behaviour to protect the prey is necessary. I saw a clear example of this when my collared female leopard killed an adult male impala, too large for her to carry up a tree; as a result two hyaenas took it over before she had fed on it for more than a few hours, whereas it would normally have provided her with food for several days.

This female had a female cub, about eighteen months old, and I had radio-collars on both animals for a while. The cub was in the process of becoming independent, and the hunting strategies of the two animals contrasted markedly. At first the mother made a fairly large kill every few days, usually an impala or a gazelle. She would carry it up a tree, feed on it for a few hours, and then go and find the cub and lead her to the kill. Both animals fed intermittently at the kill until it was consumed within a day or two, when the leopards would separate again. When she was on her own, the young female spent much of her time trying to catch various small animals such as hares, hyraxes, dikdiks and various birds; her mother rarely bothered with such small food items. The cub was clearly still dependent on her mother for part of her food supply at this stage. Although she tried to catch larger prey, she did not succeed until two months later, when she and her mother no longer met one another.

Unlike lions or cheetahs, when leopards start feeding they frequently pluck some of the hair or feathers of their prey, pulling out several mouthfuls at a time with their incisor teeth and letting them drop to the ground. They do not usually eat the skin of larger animals such as gazelles, impalas or reedbucks, and the decaying skin with parts of the skeleton attached may remain dangling from a branch for weeks after the leopard has finished feeding from it. Thus I would be much more likely to detect large leopard kills of this sort than small ones, such as a starling, which I saw consumed within ten minutes.

Leopards habitually catch and eat a wide variety of prey animals, much wider than do lions. My list of 150 leopard kills from the Serengeti, for example, is made up of over 30 different species, whereas

70 A large leopard cub looks at its potential meal (an impala fawn) which its mother
has hung over the branches of a tree, out of reach of hyaenas and lions

a similar number of lion kills would be likely to comprise fewer than a
dozen different species. The difference, I think, is because being both
solitary and smaller, leopards feed on smaller prey species, and there
are almost always more smaller species in a habitat.

The smallest prey I saw caught was the starling, by my young female
leopard, although I also saw her trying, without success, to catch
several minute birds. Patrick Hamilton found that the leopards he was
studying in Tsavo National Park fed extensively on rodents and other
small animals; Tsavo contains far fewer gazelle-sized animals than the
Serengeti. At the other end of the scale, the largest leopard kills I
recorded were wildebeest calves and zebra foals; these had been caught
mainly by adult male leopards, whose much greater size and strength
are presumably necessary to be able to kill such large prey without too
much risk of injury. The prey species most commonly caught by
leopards in the Serengeti are impalas and gazelles. On the whole these
are of a size which provides food for a leopard for two or three days, yet
they are not too heavy to be carried up trees. The relative number of
these two abundant species caught depends on their distribution:

impalas are common in the woodlands throughout the year, while gazelles come into the woodlands in the dry season only, and tend to stay mainly at the edges. Adults of the other smaller ungulate species in the leopards' habitat are also taken, such as reedbuck, bushbuck, duiker, dikdik and steinbok; so too, when available, are the young of the larger ungulates – zebra, wildebeest and topi.

Leopards in the Serengeti only occasionally kill primates such as baboons and vervet monkeys. The oft-repeated statement that baboons are leopards' favourite food is not borne out by my observations in this region, nor in Tsavo. Certainly in some places leopards kill baboons, and in those places there is usually little other food for them. But in the Serengeti, where there is a wide range of alternative food species, the leopards almost always avoided the baboons when I saw the two species meet. If one of a troop of these monkeys saw a leopard it started giving loud alarm barks which alerted the whole troop. The adult male

72 An infant baboon takes a ride in jockey fashion on its mother's back. Contrary to popular belief, baboons are not the leopard's favourite food, because male baboons will co-operate in defending the troop

71 An adult male impala, the antelope species which lives in woodland and provides leopards with a large proportion of the latter's food supply

baboons, however, did not flee: they faced and threatened the leopard. With their canine teeth as large and their jaws as powerful as a leopard's, baboons will unite in attacking the predator. If a leopard came across a single defenceless female or young baboon it would doubtless kill it, but usually the baboons' organized social behaviour prevents this. Even when I saw an encounter between a pair of leopards and a baboon troop, it was the former which moved away, but perhaps because they were preoccupied with mating at the time.

Leopards stalk and catch a number of birds, both large and small. My radio-collared animals, particularly the young female, stalked several tiny birds which were near the ground, as well as the larger ground-dwelling guinea fowl, francolins, spurfowl and storks. Leopards also managed to climb up to two vulture nests and take the chick from each. Birds and monkeys both have colour vision; leopards presumably require better camouflage and concealment for catching them than lions need to catch their colour-blind prey.

A surprisingly large number of animals which became the victims of leopards were themselves carnivores. Lion cub, cheetah, hyaena, wild dog, jackal, serval cat, wild cat, mongoose and python all featured in the relatively small number of leopard kills recorded, and twice I saw a genet nearly join them but escape up a tree in time. Why predators should be apparently subject to an extra high risk of being preyed upon themselves is not clear: perhaps it is because their activity times tend to coincide with those of leopards, or because they are less well adapted for rapid fleeing. It is not surprising that leopards should catch some of them, but it is puzzling that they should take so many. Like most carnivores, leopards will kill more than they need if easy opportunities present themselves. At one time when wildebeest with calves were migrating in large numbers through Seronera, I saw a bloated leopard there with three calves' carcasses all largely uneaten hanging from the branches of the tree in which it lay.

SOCIAL SYSTEM AND BEHAVIOUR

In contrast with lions, but like the other cat species, leopards are basically solitary animals: they are almost always alone. No animal, of course, can be completely solitary. Females must at times be associated with males for mating, and with their offspring while they are rearing them. In lions we saw that females associate together often, and sometimes almost permanently, and that adult males often associate with one another, and with their offspring. None of this happens in leopards, and I very rarely saw two adults together, even of different sexes.

Leopards appear to be basically territorial. Each individual is found within a circumscribed range which is largely exclusive of others, at least of the same sex. My three radio-collared leopards each stayed within an area of about five square miles. Only one of these was adult, however, and she was a female. In Tsavo, Patrick Hamilton found that a female leopard occupied a territory of about the same size, while males used areas which were one-and-a-half to four times as large; the males' territories generally overlapped one another rather little, but they completely overlapped that of the female. It seems likely that the leopard's territorial system is like that discovered for the similarly solitary puma in North America, in that the terrain is divided up into two distinct mosaics superimposed one on top of the other. There is a mosaic of separate adjacent female territories which may overlap one another to some extent. On top of this there is a mosaic of male territories which are larger and which probably overlap less. Thus a male leopard's territory may contain the whole or part of the territories of two, three or even four different females; on the other hand, a female's territory may extend over a part of the territories of two or even three males, or it may be contained entirely within that of only one male. This is in marked contrast with lions, where the territory boundaries of males and females roughly coincide.

The territories are probably defended when necessary. Patrick Hamilton found evidence that quite serious fighting between males sometimes occurred. Leopards of both sexes also scent-mark their territories, presumably indicating their ownership by doing so. The urine-marking behaviour is fairly similar to that described in lions in its two basic types. My female leopard marked much more often than any lioness I watched, and in a more athletic manner. Her commonest method was to approach a thick horizontal branch or fallen tree trunk some three to six feet from the ground. She sniffed at its underside for several seconds, then rubbed her face against it, often having to stand on her hind legs to do so. She then walked forward or turned to bring her rear end to the point she had sniffed at, and with tail held vertically projected a brief spray of urine at the branch. Thus this upward marking is similar to urine spraying by male lions, though it is rarely used by lionesses. Male lions, however, choose a small bush and spray onto the leaves, in contrast to the leopards I observed who chose

73 A leopard sitting in the fork of a tree scratches at its neck with a hind paw

horizontal or sloping branches and fallen or standing tree trunks. Leopards also sometimes performed the downward form of urine-marking while scraping their hind feet alternately, which is the commonest form of marking by lions. It is likely that many of these marking sites have been marked before, by the same or by other individuals. The scent deposited probably indicates to the next comer both who passed by there before and how long ago it was. In some places leopards apparently also rake their claws through the bark of tree trunks and so leave another signal of their presence, but neither Hamilton nor I found much sign of this in East Africa. Nonetheless, as the leopard moves around its territory it is continually picking up information, updating it and adding new information, in a world of scent maps from which we humans are excluded.

For most of the time a leopard is a very silent animal, both in the way it moves and vocally. Its long distance call sounds rather like the noise of a rough saw being drawn back and forth about ten times while cutting through wood. It does not carry nearly as far as a lion roar, nor is it produced nearly as often. Both sexes can make this call. Males apparently use it as a way of proclaiming ownership of their territory, or perhaps advertising themselves to females. The only times I heard any of my radio-collared animals call was when the adult female was separated from her cub (which I had immobilized to radio-collar it), and then repeatedly when she was in oestrus but without a male in attendance. In both these cases the call was being used to make contact, not to keep other animals away.

Most leopard calling occurs at night and around dawn, the time when leopards are mainly active and moving around their territories. During the middle of the day they are inactive, resting in the shade in a thicket, stream bed or kopje, or up in a tree, where they lie draped over a branch, their spotted coat blending well with the mottled shade (especially when in a yellow-barked fever tree), and their limbs and tail hanging limply down on either side. Often it is a glimpse of the long tail dangling down which first gives away the leopard's presence. They do not in fact lie in trees as often as is supposed; but if they are lying in a thicket they are most unlikely to be found at all, and therefore there is an enormous bias in favour of sightings in trees.

REPRODUCTION

There does not appear to be a breeding season for leopards, at any rate in East Africa near the equator. When a female is in oestrus, mating takes place repeatedly for a few days. Soliciting and mating by my radio-collared female were very similar to the pattern I saw so frequently in lions, but mating is rarely observed in leopards, which suggests that it is more efficient than in lions. The gestation period is about three months. The usual litter size in the Serengeti seems to be two cubs, but these are not seen until they are about two months old, and it is possible that early losses take place. In the Serengeti, at least, usually only one cub is still surviving by the age of a year or so. Some mothers do rear two or very occasionally three cubs, but this is rare. I have almost no information on the causes of leopard cub mortality.

The young are spotted from birth but of a greyer hue overall than adults. They seem to be more independent and self-sufficient than lions from quite an early age, and are less likely to be with their mother than a lion cub of comparable age. Lion cubs follow their mother and other adult members of the pride who are hunting; if they did not they would get no food from most small kills. A mother leopard, on the other hand, leaves her cubs behind when she goes off to hunt; if she is successful, she hides the prey and then fetches her young. Later, when the cub is older, it makes its own private efforts at hunting, as I described, and manages to supply some of its own food. Lions at a comparable stage would be participating in co-operative hunts but unable to capture prey animals themselves.

When her cub was about twenty-one months old, my radio-collared female came on heat again for several days, and mated intermittently. After that I never saw her meet her offspring again; once she passed her dozing daughter forty yards away, but neither noticed the other. It was around this time that the daughter began to succeed in catching larger prey animals, and it seemed that she had now acquired her hunting skills by her own trial and error. By comparison, it would appear likely that young lions learn to hunt successfully in part by watching experienced adults doing so.

The young female leopard remained in her mother's territory. Since both animals urine-marked as they travelled around in it, each probably knew the other's whereabouts reasonably well. I had to remove the radio-collars at the end of my study period, so I do not know how long the daughter continued to use her mother's area. However, from the long-term records of known individuals at Seronera, it seems that daughters have generally settled in the vicinity in which they were brought up, appropriating part of their mothers' range, and probably producing their own cubs there by the age of about three years.

A young male of about two-and-a-half to three years old was fortunate enough to wear one of my radio-collars for a few months. He was fully independent and seemed to be proficient at hunting for himself. Nevertheless, he often joined an elderly adult female, especially at

74 A leopard and her two cubs. Leopards rarely manage to rear more than one. Note the white underside to the tip of her tail, which acts as a conspicuous signal and flag for her cubs to follow

75 A young leopard, camouflaged amid its surroundings, yawns and displays its sharp white teeth. Note the enormously long whiskers

night. I suspect that she was his mother, and that they came together more often than normal because she did not have a subsequent litter of cubs. He usually appeared more eager than she to be in contact: he would run after her as she walked, rub his side along her flank and then shove her sideways with his rump, while his long tail rested over her back. She seldom responded other than with a mild retracting of her lips in protest, but occasionally the two animals groomed one another's head and neck. Shortly before the male's collar stopped functioning he was wandering more, and thereafter I was unable to find him again. I suspect that he was driven out by a fully adult male who from that time I started to see regularly in the area.

Again from the long-term records of individual leopards at Seronera, it seems that young males, unlike their sisters, do not remain in the region in which they were born, but there is no information on where they are likely to go or why they leave. Emigration by males from their birthplaces would account for the fact that almost all of the least timid leopards in the Serengeti are females, who have grown up in areas with tourist vehicles to which they have become accustomed. By contrast, males immigrating there from other areas would be afraid of and hide from vehicles. Also, if males maintain larger territories than females, there will of course be fewer resident males than females in any area, perhaps only half as many. It is not known whether there are many non-territorial or nomadic male leopards, or whether males suffer a higher mortality rate than females.

There is very little information either on how long leopards usually live in the wild. I have identified individuals shown in old photographs and magazine articles, and have found two females who lived for at least ten and twelve years. One of them is still alive at the time of writing, her worn ears and heavy face betraying her age. In the Serengeti leopard deaths have been caused by lions, by fights with other leopards and by injury when falling from a height when a rotten branch gave way. The old female of twelve had a large hernia when I last saw her. Doubtless many others die a peaceful natural death, unseen in a thicket.

INTERACTIONS WITH OTHER SPECIES

As it moves around, a leopard encounters a large number of other animal species. Some of these become leopard food, as I have already

160

described in the section on hunting and feeding, but with others, particularly other predators, the interactions are less one-sided.

Relations with lions I refer to in Chapter 11. Cheetahs usually avoid leopards, although I have twice seen young female leopards having to escape up a tree from adult cheetahs, which cannot climb; on the whole the habitats of the two species are different. Although spotted hyaenas sometimes fall prey to leopards, they usually drive them off. A leopard can sprint much faster than a hyaena; it appears to know this, for a leopard merely avoids the close proximity of a hyaena, rather than fleeing from it. Hyaenas, like dogs, are totally unable to climb trees, while leopards are arboreally agile, and it is for this reason that in most regions where spotted hyaenas are common the leopards have developed the habit of carrying their kills up into safety. This habit is reported to be much less prevalent in Asia.

Jackals, being far smaller, are no match for a leopard, but nor can they usually be caught by a leopard in reasonably open country. Jackals can run fast and long, and can dodge nimbly; in consequence, when they encounter a leopard they often stay within thirty yards of it, repeatedly making their loud, sharp, high-pitched barks. They may persist in doing so for hours until the leopard departs; in one instance a jackal kept it up all night. My radio-collared female was once apparently driven away from her resting place by a jackal's incessant barking at her from fifteen yards away. Twice she turned and rushed at it, but the jackal kept away from her without difficulty, only to resume its yapping and close following as she moved off to the seclusion of a larger thicket.

A number of large ungulates are invulnerable to leopards by virtue of their size. Giraffes usually ignore them, although once I saw a huge male being put to flight by a subadult male leopard: the giraffe stood watching the leopard's stealthy approach but his nerve failed and he turned and loped off, with the leopard running alongside. Motionless or running, he was certainly far too large for the leopard to have tackled. I saw buffalo bulls chase a leopard on a number of occasions, but the encounters were all short because the leopard easily eluded the buffalo, which did not follow up its lunge. I got the impression that the leopard was merely inquisitive, and was approaching the buffalo closely just out of curiosity. An adult female warthog out in the open showed no fear of a leopard twenty to thirty yards away, and followed a similar distance behind when the leopard walked off; but other warthogs with their vulnerable piglets kept a much greater distance away.

Once I watched a banded mongoose escape death by leopard by its spirited defence. From the base of a bush it lunged repeatedly with its sharp teeth at the nose or paws of the much larger leopard, and for half an hour it managed to thwart the latter's attempts to seize its body. Presumably the small amount of meat the leopard would have obtained from the mongoose would not have made up for a painful bite, and the larger predator eventually left.

Tsetse flies troubled leopards considerably. Their victim would repeatedly twitch its very mobile skin, flick its long tail around its body and try unsuccessfully to bite at the offending fly with its teeth. After a while it would often walk hurriedly or trot away into a shaded thicket where it was less bothered by the irritating insects.

Man's relationship with leopards is a complicated one. Leopards are so secretive that they can survive close to human habitation without their existence being realized, except when they take occasional dogs or chickens. A few become regular scavengers around dustbins and rubbish dumps, as hyaenas do, but generally they keep well out of the way of humans. People can get badly scratched or bitten if a leopard is cornered or trapped, but man-eating is extremely rare. There have been famous cases of man-eating leopards in India, but scarcely any in Africa.

By contrast, men deliberately kill thousands of leopards each year. A small proportion of these are shot for sport, and many more are killed for their skins. To watch at close quarters, as I have, a wild leopard living its normal life while wearing its skin, so beautifully suited to leopards, would cure most people of any desire to wear that skin themselves. Yet many thousands of people still apparently want to clothe their bodies with bits of *Panthera pardus* epidermis. Norman Myers estimated recently that at present about 50,000 leopards a year die for the fur trade. The figure is so high partly because of the very wasteful methods of killing the natural owners of those skins; and most of it is officially illegal. The killing also tends to be concentrated in the areas where leopards are most accessible, and as a result they have become almost or completely wiped out from those areas. If it were considered desirable, the leopard populations of Africa could certainly sustain an offtake of many thousands of skins, *provided* that this offtake was more evenly spread. Much better legal enforcement would be needed, and stronger international agreements between all the importing and exporting countries, and the latter could receive a much greater and sustained income from skin dealings which were legal and control-

76 One of the oldest Seronera leopards dozes on a branch. I recognized individual leopards by the patterns of small spots on the head, and could trace their life-histories from old photographs. Note her tattered worn ears

led. Meanwhile public feeling in the importing countries, especially in the West, should I hope gradually diminish the demand and so the prices offered for skins, and thus reduce the incentive for poachers to operate. These changes should lessen the intense pressure on many leopard populations in theoretically protected wildlife areas.

In agricultural areas the position is different. Leopards in such areas are exterminated partly because they are hunted for fur, but mainly because of conflicts with farming. They take only a very small toll of domestic livestock, but the farmer who loses a calf or a kid to a leopard naturally tends to take measures to prevent it happening again if he can ('naturally' because that is human nature, rather than because it is justifiable). It is easy for an African farmer to obtain insecticides which he can put into pieces of meat as bait for leopards; such compounds kill any animal which eats the bait, including leopards which may or may not be the one who is the stock-robber. As a result, leopards have disappeared, or are fast doing so, from most agricultural areas, as has happened to predators over much of Europe and North America for similar reasons which are regrettable but understandable. Large predators such as leopards do not mix well with intensive agriculture, but in pockets of uncultivated land they might be beneficial in helping to keep down the numbers of rodents and other agricultural pests.

Overall, however, the long-term future prospects of the leopard species in the wild are not bleak. Some thousands will be able to survive in isolated populations in strictly controlled national parks in Africa. The leopard's adaptability means that it can survive at high altitudes, in semi-arid areas and in rocky country, in all of which agriculture is largely impossible. There will be many undisturbed pieces of land of this sort for many years. Able to feed on any or all of an enormous variety of small prey species, leopards are relatively little influenced by changes in vegetation, climate or prey animals. Man may eventually exterminate lions or cheetahs in the wild by depriving them of the wide areas stocked with large prey animals which these species need for their survival. It would take him a great deal longer to wipe out the adaptable, unspecialized, beautiful leopard from its wide variety of habitats, and one hopes that he will not be so greedy and misguided as to try to do so.

8 · The cheetah

The cheetah is the second species of large cat to be found in the lion's environment. It is a relatively scarce animal, more common on the plains than in my main woodland study area in the Serengeti, for woodlands are essentially the habitat of the lion and leopard. Nevertheless, I watched any cheetahs I came across and established identity cards for them as I did for lions and leopards.

APPEARANCE

Whereas the leopard represents the typical adaptable generalized large cat, the cheetah is at the other extreme: it is totally specialized for speed in the open. It is well known to be the fastest running animal there is over its chosen distance, and its appearance underlines this ability. All unnecessary weight has been eliminated in the course of its evolution. Thus a cheetah's head is smaller in relation to the size of the body than in any other cat, and its whole body is slender and elongated; this gives it a wonderfully functional beauty as well as a greyhound-like appearance, which should not be surprising as greyhounds too have been selected for speed, although by man rather than by Nature. As in a greyhound, the flexible backbone bends and straightens as the cheetah runs, giving extra length to each stride; it has been calculated that even a legless cheetah could 'run' at five miles an hour just by the movement of its spine!

The cheetah's un-catlike characteristics are reflected in its taxonomy. The lion, tiger, leopard and jaguar all belong to the genus *Panthera*. Of the other cats which approach the cheetah in size, the

77 A well-fed cheetah at rest

puma, snow leopard and lynx are all closely related to *Felis*, the genus typical of most of the small cats. Yet the cheetah is closely related to neither, but must have diverged at an early stage in the evolution of the cat family. There are no other members of its genus, *Acinonyx*. All other cats retract their claws into sheaths when not in use; only the cheetah is unable to do this, and so the ends of its blunt claws leave impressions when the cheetah walks, making doglike footprints. The dogs are, of course, runners while the cats are usually stalkers.

A cheetah is about the same size as a leopard, higher but slimmer, and therefore weighs between one-third and a half as much as a lion, or around one hundredweight. The sexes are similar in size, with males little larger but of slightly heavier build; there is nowhere near the same degree of sexual dimorphism as in either lions or leopards. A cheetah stands only 2½–3 ft high, and its total length is some 7 ft, of which about 2½ ft is tail.

The name cheetah comes from a Sanskrit word meaning 'speckled bodied'. The whole fawn-coloured body is covered with bold round black spots with smaller faint ones interspersed among them; they are not arranged in rosettes as in leopards. The tail has alternate rings of black and white, and culminates in a white tip; when a cheetah sprinted, from far away I could sometimes see this conspicuous white fleck waving, and I presume it helped her cubs, if she had any, to keep

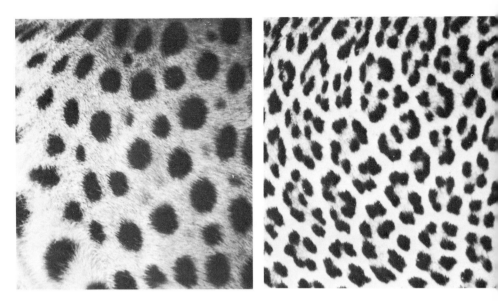

78 a&b Spots of cheetah and leopard compared. The cheetah has mainly large round black spots with a few small faint ones interspersed among them. Most of the leopard's body is covered with 'rosettes', each consisting of a few spots arranged in a small irregular ring

track of where she went. Cheetahs have a very striking and characteristic black tear streak which runs down from the inside corner of the eye to the outside edge of the mouth. The spots on the cheeks are small. I found that each cheetah had a different spot arrangement, and so I could use these spot patterns to distinguish between different individuals. I would guess that as with the leopard the same applies to the bigger spots elsewhere on the body, but the latter have the same problems over stretching, reference points and other people's photographs. For a cheetah lying at rest or in long grass the sides of the face are the most convenient parts, and sometimes the only parts, of the body I could photograph. Again as with leopards, and rather surprisingly, the patterns of spots on the two sides of the face are not identical, so when I identified the individual from one side, I could verify it independently by looking at the other.

HUNTING METHODS

In order to feed herself ('she' because most of the cheetahs I watched were females), a cheetah has first to find a suitable victim and then to

79 An adult male Thomson's gazelle, the species which provides more cheetah meals than any other

get within reasonably close range of it. Typically she will be in a region of open country with relatively little cover. She moves around in search of possible prey, often stopping and squatting in a very characteristic upright posture on her haunches, or climbing onto a termite mound or low branch and scanning the countryside for gazelles or other prey species. Having seen one, she approaches the gazelle, openly when it is far away, then more cautiously as she gets closer. As long as the gazelle is feeding or otherwise occupied the cheetah comes towards it; she has a curious stalking posture with head held low and legs looking remarkably stiff. When the gazelle looks up, the cheetah freezes like a statue. As she gets closer she may hold the body lower, but her approach is different from the stalk-and-crouch approach of a leopard. Soon, as the chances that she will be detected rise, she speeds up, to a gliding trot, then a run, and finally a flat-out sprint. By this time the prey has usually seen her coming and is in headlong flight with the cheetah racing after it. Both are very swift runners. A cheetah can achieve a speed of about seventy miles per hour and a gazelle nearly as much. The gazelle runs straight at first, but as the cheetah gets close to it, it may try to jink or turn sharply. This sometimes makes the cheetah overshoot, but often it means that she can cut the corner and gain further on her intended victim. The chase slows down a bit as both animals begin to tire and as the gazelle circles and dodges more. Eventually the cheetah manages to make contact and brings the prey down either by landing a paw on the prey's rump or by sweeping its hind legs from under it. She immediately holds onto the throat of the prey, which dies of strangulation within a minute or two, because after such exertion its need for air is enormous. The cheetah rarely starts to feed at once; more often she squats on her haunches panting hard for many minutes, a clear sign of her considerable exertion.

Despite her speed, a cheetah faces considerable problems in catching her prey. If prey are scarce, the problem of finding animals to hunt means that she must often cover large distances. But if prey are common they tend to warn one another of her approach. Any antelope which sees a distant cheetah snorts and watches the predator. Potential victims are alerted by the noise and by the predator-watching posture of those animals which have seen her. A healthy adult gazelle is safe if it stays more than about fifty yards from her, and a travelling cheetah is

80 An adult cheetah drags to cover the gazelle which it has just caught after a high-speed chase

often followed by a tail of apparently inquisitive gazelles or wildebeest. The latter, if adult, are too large for cheetah, and I have seen them following only about ten to twenty yards behind one. She appeared to object to her retinue and charged them several times; each time the wildebeest snorted, wheeled and galloped away from her, only to resume their following when she continued on her way.

Even without such followers, it is difficult in open country for a cheetah to make her way undetected to within about forty yards of an unsuspecting prey animal. She has to get as close as this because she can use her tremendous speed only over the relatively short distance of two or three hundred yards. Richard Taylor has shown with cheetahs trained to run in a treadmill that much more heat is generated in the cheetah's muscles during a sprint than can possibly be dissipated at the time by sweating, panting or any other means, so its body temperature rises rapidly, to around 105°F; the cheetah cannot run any further because if it did its brain would be cooked!

Gazelles, which also have to cope with long-distance runners such as wild dogs, do not suffer from this over-heating problem. They have a special network of blood vessels at the base of the brain, where the temperature of blood on its way to the brain is lowered by cooler blood which has come from the nasal passages where evaporation is taking place. Thus, provided it is not overtaken too quickly, a gazelle can outdistance a cheetah because of its superior ability to deal with the problem of overheating.

Compared with lions' hunting, cheetahs' chases are more likely to be successful. At least half the times a cheetah sprints she catches her prey. This may indicate not so much greater efficiency on the part of the cheetah as less optimism. Her chases are far more exhausting for her than lions' hunts are, so she probably does not start a sprint unless she is more certain of success than a lion can be. Her high success rate is also caused partly by the fact that she tends to select fawns, which cannot run as fast as adults and which can almost always be caught. When gazelles were abundant, I saw cheetahs hunting simply by walking through gazelle concentrations until they spotted small fawns which they then started to chase at a lower speed for several hundred yards. Sometimes a group of two or more male cheetahs travel and hunt together, which enables them to capture wildebeest calves. A wildebeest cow can often defend her calf against a single cheetah, but if there are a pair of them, one can drive her off while the other deals with her calf.

170

In the Serengeti, the great majority of cheetahs' kills are gazelles, mainly Thomson's gazelles, as these are smaller and at least ten times as abundant as Grant's. Although a cheetah's diet also includes some hares, wildebeest calves and impalas, the range of prey species taken is much narrower than for leopards. The main reason for this is habitat: cheetahs tend to live in open country where there are large numbers of prey animals, but few species. I rarely encountered cheetahs in the woodlands, but when I did they were hunting or feeding mainly on impalas, which are also the main leopard food there. In Nairobi and Kruger National Parks, too, the cheetahs feed mainly on the abundant impala. Woodlands provide a wider range of different kinds of ecological niche, for example the streamside vegetation and the kopjes, and the leopard's method of hunting is better suited to catching the wider range of species which occupy these niches. Only stealth, not speed, is effective for catching birds. Also, because cheetahs do all their hunting by day and are inactive at night, they do not encounter some of the nocturnal species which contribute to the leopard's diet.

Cheetahs' kills are relatively small: a Thomson's gazelle fawn weighs only a pound or two, and an adult about forty pounds. Particularly if a female cheetah has several large cubs with her, she has to kill quite often, and in fact does so most days. Single cheetahs, by contrast, catch

81 Two large cheetah cubs feed on a gazelle fawn, while their mother who is still panting from exhaustion keeps an eye open for larger predators

prey only every two or three days on average, depending of course on the size of the victim. If they catch a large animal, they eat their fill and make no attempt to guard or store the remains for another meal. I can think of almost no way in which they could do so effectively. Thus cheetahs do not use the meat they have caught as efficiently as the other predators, leaving a larger edible proportion on each kill.

SOCIAL ORGANIZATION

Female cheetahs are essentially solitary as adults. I only once saw two adult females together; and only once did I see an adult male with an adult female, although obviously they must come together to mate. By contrast, adult males may be alone or in pairs or occasionally threes. Such pairs of adult males were generally assumed to be brothers from the same litter, but by recognizing cheetahs individually by their cheek spots, and by keeping long-term records of those individuals, I was able to show that in fact they were not necessarily related. Two adult males from different parents may come together and form stable and long-lasting partnerships. Teamwork enables them to catch some larger prey such as wildebeest calves, as described, but on the whole it means that they must hunt more often, for they each get less food from each kill. Also, it may enable them to overpower single rival males: Alan Root has taken some superb film of a pair of male cheetahs fighting with and defeating a solitary one.

Most groups of apparently adult cheetahs turn out, in fact, to be a mother and her nearly independent offspring. A group of seven large cheetahs which I saw several times in the Serengeti was composed of a well-known female, the five cubs she had successfully reared (an unusually large number) to subadulthood, and another subadult which had attached itself to the group at a late stage. Although the young animals tolerated the last completely, the adult female usually kept the hanger-on a few yards from the rest of the group when they were all at rest; but at a kill she seemed unable to distinguish it among the other five large animals all feeding busily, so it was able to secure a food supply. Even when subadults have become independent of their mother, at about eighteen months old, they often stay together; the females do so for only a few months until they become pregnant, but brothers may keep one another company for longer.

Cheetahs, like leopards, are probably solitary because their prey

172

82 Two cheetahs, damp after a thunderstorm. I recognized individual cheetahs by the pattern of small spots on the cheeks, which is different in every animal

animals are small. Unlike leopards, however, they do not stay within fixed territories. I have little information on how far they go, other than my occasional observations of individuals at places at least twenty or thirty miles apart. It will take much more work, and perhaps radio-tracking of cheetahs, to discover how large a range individuals use, and what this depends on; George and Lory Frame are carrying out such work in the Serengeti now. Cheetahs appear to move in a rather haphazard way, going to where the migratory gazelles are abundant and often staying for several days in one part of their range before moving on to another part. There seems to be little territorial behaviour, since the ranges of many different individuals overlap enormously. An adult cheetah avoids another if it sees one, rather than trying to drive it away. It may leave faeces on termite mounds, but these seem merely to indicate the cheetah's presence rather than to show possession. And cheetahs do not have a loud call like leopards or particularly lions; they make a birdlike chirping noise when separated from one another, and quite a loud moaning sound when close to lions or leopards, but the rest of their noises are soft and seldom made. Unlike lions and leopards, cheetahs can and do purr like the small cats.

Mating in cheetahs has very rarely been seen and never by me. Since they obviously do it, the process is probably efficient compared with lions where it is so often observed. There is no particular breeding season, and cheetah cubs may be born at almost any time of year, after a gestation period of three months. Their litter sizes are larger than in lions or leopards, usually containing four to six cubs. These are of surprising and delightful appearance, their flanks and belly being so dark-spotted as to look almost black, while they have a cape of long greyish hairs on the neck, shoulders and back. The cubs are born and kept hidden in a small thicket or under a bush, and are moved from one such hiding place to another every few days. Cub mortality is quite high during the first month, much of it probably due to predation. A cheetah cannot defend her cubs against lions, leopards or hyaenas, all of which would kill and eat any cubs they came across; so would jackals if they discovered a litter of small cubs without the cheetah in attendance. She has to leave them to go hunting, and on her return she suckles them and also regurgitates food for them, another characteristic which is doglike rather than catlike.

When they are about four weeks old the cubs leave cover and follow their mother. They are not very mobile at this stage, and still vulnerable. About 50 per cent of them die in the next three months, but those who survive develop rapidly. By the age of a few months there is only a faint watermark left to remind one of the birth coat pattern, and the body is beginning to elongate towards the adult cheetah's appearance. Like all young cats, cheetah cubs play a great deal, and I was struck by the way their playing consists of more chasing and less wrestling than I have seen among either lion cubs or domestic kittens.

The mother is no longer anchored to the vicinity of the birth place now, and the group may roam over large distances in their search for food. The cubs stay behind as the female goes ahead to stalk and chase prey animals. As they get older they stay put less, may go ahead of the female, and are liable by their playing to disturb the prey, thus generally making hunting more difficult for their mother. They watch her hunting, and presumably learn from it. As soon as they see her make a kill they run up and start feeding at once; if they do not she calls them with her sharp chirping call. Occasionally if she catches a gazelle fawn she does not kill it but releases it alive for her cubs to chase, much as domestic cats do, but something which I saw only once among lions.

By the time the young are about a year-and-a-half old they are full sized, although not quite as heavily built as adults. At this age they separate from their mother, sometimes most abruptly: one day they are with her and the next they are on their own; it is in marked contrast with the gradually increasing independence from her mother that I saw with my young leopard. The young cheetahs now have to rely entirely on their own speed and whatever skill or experience they have developed. They certainly seem much less efficient than adults, and their usually lean appearance also suggests that they experience some difficulty in finding or catching food.

As already mentioned, the subadults may stay together as a group for a while, until the females separate around the time when they become pregnant. Their first litter is born at about two years old, which is a year younger than for lions and as would be expected from a considerably smaller animal. A mother who has successfully reared one or more cubs to independence usually becomes pregnant fairly soon after that, and thus should produce cubs at roughly two year intervals, as lions do. However, if her cubs die, at any stage, she often mates and conceives again soon afterwards. I had records of a cheetah producing her next litter only four months after her previous unsuccessful one – much more quickly than in lions, although their gestation period is about the same length.

MORTALITY

No one knows yet how long cheetahs usually live in the wild. I hope that after a few more years the individual cheetahs' long-term records, which I started in the Serengeti and which have been continued and greatly expanded by the Frames, will provide this information. Although dead adults are rarely found, there must be a fairly high level of adult mortality because the survival of cheetah cubs seems moderately good after the early stages, and yet the population does not appear to be increasing. In fact, considering how successful cheetahs are both at hunting and at rearing cubs, there are surprisingly few of them: the Serengeti area which holds about two thousand lions has only about a tenth as many cheetahs.

Why are cheetahs not more common? I would imagine that life for adult cheetahs is considerably more difficult than for lions, for several reasons. Their method of hunting is much more exhausting and, because the prey animals they catch are relatively small, cheetahs have to hunt more often than lions do. A pregnant cheetah probably finds it even more difficult to make its kills, while an injured one is quite likely to starve. One female with four cubs of three or four months old was lame and stiff in her left front leg; both she and her cubs were unusually thin and I thought all were in danger of starving to death. Fortunately she seemed to be exceptionally skilful at making kills despite her lack of speed, and she just managed to rear all four of her cubs. By contrast, an injured lioness and her cubs would have little problem obtaining their meals from prey killed by other members of their pride. Lions, too, can use food killed by other predators, because with their greater size they can deprive almost all other predators or scavengers of a carcass. Cheetahs with their smaller size and feeble weapons cannot do this: they do not rob other predators of food, and nor do they scavenge from carcasses of animals which have died of natural causes.

The mortality of cubs is high, but it is difficult to determine how high without close and continuous observation of the same individuals. On a number of occasions I saw a female cheetah who was either pregnant or lactating, but there were no signs of any cubs when I saw her next. If, as often happens, the whole litter is lost early on, I might never know that a female did actually produce one. All I saw of one litter which was apparently discovered by an unknown small predator was a scattering of hair, seven little paws uneaten and a third dying cub. Another cheetah lost all of her first three litters at an early stage, and may also have produced other unsuccessful litters which I never detected, before eventually rearing five out of the six cubs which she produced when she was just over five years old.

The causes of this high but irregular cub mortality are obscure. Possibly disease is important. Predation almost certainly is, although it is rarely actually observed. One litter disappeared suddenly and was never seen again; the same night hyaenas were digging at a burrow nearby, and probably came across the cheetah cubs in the course of their activity. The only case of predation on cheetahs I witnessed accounted for an eight-day-old cub. Its mother was in the process of moving her litter to a new hiding place a few hundred yards away, carrying each small cub in her mouth. Suddenly she was ambushed at close range by two young lionesses; the cheetah fled at once but dropped her cub as she did so, and one of the lionesses seized and killed it instantly. They would probably have eaten it, but I recovered the corpse to examine it. Its mother moaned loudly several times and then returned gradually and secretively to the remainder of her litter. She typically, and understandably, made no attempt to defend her ill-fated cub against the much larger lionesses.

INTERACTIONS WITH OTHER SPECIES

Those two lionesses had been specializing in robbing cheetahs, partly perhaps because one of them was young and the other slightly lame, thus making them both less efficient at hunting the sparse prey in the area. A cheetah catching its prey in daylight in open country is often visible from a long way off. If a lion sees the event, it usually runs up and appropriates the kill. The cheetah can do nothing about its loss because it is too small to resist such robbery, too weak and probably too exhausted after its hunt to run off with its prey, and unable to carry the prey up a tree as leopards do. It merely moans and moves away. Hyaenas, too, rob cheetahs of their kills; although not much larger, hyaenas are much stronger and better armed, and cheetahs cannot risk injury. Cheetahs' specialization for speed, which enables them to capture their prey, means also that they cannot defend it.

Even if the capture was not observed by lions or hyaenas, it or the resultant carcass may well be spotted by vultures soaring overhead. A feeding cheetah is soon attended by a growing group of vultures. Their arrival often attracts lions or hyaenas, and as though aware of this the cheetah becomes increasingly nervous. At the same time it is getting fuller and so less hungry, while the vultures become bolder. They often start to press nearer in a body, and sometimes appear to drive the nearly full cheetah from its kill by their approach. At other times a cheetah will rush at vultures which come too close, and keep them away from its kill. Two young cheetahs were not afraid of the vultures on the ground close to their kill, and occasionally ran at them; yet when that happened the frightened vultures took to the air in a flurry, which startled the cheetahs away again, and so the two species oscillated back and forth.

Most animals do not interact closely with cheetahs. The latter avoid all the other large predators. The bigger ungulates, such as giraffes and zebras, watch cheetahs alertly, often snorting but otherwise ignoring them. Gazelles and wildebeest often follow a cheetah. So too do jackals, making their shrill barking to the cheetah's apparent annoyance. A cheetah sometimes chases a jackal, but the latter usually has little difficulty in dodging and eluding its pursuer. On one occasion I saw a cheetah and a warthog, both adult females, threatening and circling round one another, about ten yards apart; after a couple of minutes the cheetah walked off, followed closely and steadily by the warthog which appeared to be driving off its opponent. The same cheetah had just chased a nearly full-grown female leopard, which escaped up a tree, but it is more usual for cheetahs to steer clear of leopards.

In national parks, man is another animal which tends to follow cheetahs, particularly in order to watch them hunting. Until recently cheetahs were exceedingly timid and avoided tourists' cars, keeping at distances of about two hundred yards. Now, however, in a few areas of which the Serengeti is one, they have become remarkably tolerant of vehicles. One or two females which were 'anchored' by having small cubs were the first to learn that cars did them no harm, and consequently their cubs grew up tamer still. Indeed in the Serengeti and in Nairobi Park some of the cheetahs will jump onto the bonnet and roof of a visiting car. I have often had one particular tame female sitting on the bonnet of my landrover, peering in occasionally at the movements inside or at its reflection in the windscreen, but more usually using the car as a kind of large mobile termite mound, which afforded it both a warm behind and a good view of potential prey or of the approach of other predators. This cheetah's twin sister, her two younger brothers and her own five offspring all continued the habit: I once had about a quarter of a ton of cheetah on the front and roof of my landrover.

Tourists in their cars eager to see a cheetah hunting often make it considerably more difficult for her to do so. They tend to try to follow her too closely, thereby disturbing the prey animals which she is trying to approach undetected. On the other hand the prey animals are gradually (but more slowly) also becoming accustomed to cars and therefore are less disturbed by them. One female Grant's gazelle paid with its life for failing to notice the approach, across completely flat bare ground, of a cheetah followed by a retinue of two cubs, my landrover, eight minibuses and a lorry! Overall, although my samples are small, it seems that tame cheetahs do at least as well at raising young as timid ones, and in time more areas should have such easily approachable cheetahs.

This, of course, is assuming that cheetahs are not harassed or poached by humans. In the national parks in Africa individual cheetahs are relatively safe, although the populations in those parks are small and thus are potentially vulnerable. For example, there are only

83 Cheetahs often use termite mounds as vantage points or resting places. A few cheetahs in the Serengeti have learned that car bonnets make quite good warm mobile termite mounds; one reclines on the front of my landrover

about two hundred cheetahs in the Serengeti, so if there were to occur a change in whatever factors keep the cheetah population down to such a low level, they could disappear quickly. Cheetahs require large areas with large populations of prey animals, and such areas are becoming more scarce in the world. Agriculture, cattle ranching and human hunting of wild animals all contribute to a progressive shrinking of the areas where cheetahs can survive. In this century they have become extinct in India, and almost extinct in most of the countries of the Middle East, Arabia and northern Africa. Norman Myers, who carried out a survey of their status in Africa for the International Union for the Conservation of Nature, estimated that in 1973 the world population of cheetahs was about 14,000, and that this would have shrunk to about half that number by 1980. They are now to be found almost entirely in ten countries from South Africa to Sudan, with a scattering too along the southern fringe of the Sahara. Their main habitat consists of open woodland savannah and short grasslands – often quite arid land, for cheetahs can go for long periods without drinking. The drier environments tend to have less abundant prey, but also fewer competing predators or scavengers to rob cheetahs of kills or cubs. Drier areas are also generally less favoured by an expanding human population, and so outside national parks or game reserves may provide the better long-term prospects for cheetahs.

Even there, cheetahs are not left alone, but are often trapped or shot. The Western world's wealth and its desire to cover its womenfolk in inappropriate spots provide a strong incentive for hunters and poachers to deprive cheetahs of their skins. Each year thousands of cheetah skins are still sold in the West, despite increasing legislation and growing public opinion against the practice. Even if this trade can be made to diminish, partly through more effective law enforcement, the wild cheetah population is itself dwindling. At the same time, scarcity increases the prices paid for cheetah skins, with or without their rightful owners alive inside them. There is a trade in cheetah cubs for export to become pets and exclusive status symbols. Safari parks and zoos in the West also provide a market for cheetahs, usually for adults from southern Africa. Admittedly these animals might otherwise be destroyed, for some of their captors consider them to be responsible for predation on the occasional calf or lamb. In fact, the threat posed by cheetahs to cattle ranchers' stocks is negligible, while no one believes or pretends (unlike the case of the poor maligned wolf) that cheetahs are in any way dangerous to humans themselves. Cheetahs simply do not attack people – they flee from them in the wild.

Another cause for concern about the future prospects of cheetahs is that so far they do not breed at all regularly in captivity. All the tame cheetahs which have been used for hunting in the past twenty centuries by wealthy men from Italy to India had to be caught from the wild. Only a few dozen cheetah cubs have ever been born and reared in zoos or wildlife parks, despite the thousands which have been and still are being kept. The position is improving: cheetahs are surviving better in captivity and can now occasionally be persuaded to reproduce. While it should be possible to ensure by modern techniques that the whole species does not become totally extinct, its continued existence in the wild is more dubious. In any case, the cheetah's mere existence should not be our target. We should hope that our great-grandchildren will be able, like me, to find, watch and study this elegant species in its native habitats, and to enjoy their good fortune in being able to do so.

9 · The evolution of lions

In this chapter I want to consider the probable route by which, and the reasons why, lions evolved to their present position as large successful abundant social predators. Then in the next chapter I shall discuss the ways in which natural selection is operating at the level of the individual within the lions' social system.

Since almost all other cat species are small and unsocial animals compared with lions, it is reasonable to assume that at some stage the lion's ancestor was a basically solitary smaller cat. It probably lacked both a mane and a tail tuft, characteristics which are unique to lions among the cats, but characteristics which, like sociability, the fossil record can tell us nothing about – hairs and friendships do not get fossilized and so preserved for posterity. It is not clear either whether the now extinct very large cats whose fossilized bones have been discovered were in fact lion ancestors or not. In the absence of such evidence, I consider it likely that the joint ancestor of lions and leopards looked much like the present-day unspecialized leopards. What selective pressures, then, directed the evolution of lions from this proto-lion starting point?

SOCIAL HUNTING

One of the fundamental problems which any predator faces is to catch its prey – and most of the hunts I observed, by lion, leopard or cheetah, ended in failure for the predator. There is a continuous evolutionary race between the hunted and the hunter: the prey species are subject to selection pressures making them more speedy, wary and alert over the generations: the hunter species, too, experience selective pressures which favour speed, but they also develop other methods of getting close to prey animals which prefer them at a distance. Stalking, at which all cats are skilled, is one of these methods, and lying in ambush for prey to come close is another. Hunting at night when the predator is less visible is a third way of reducing the all-important distance. Hunting where there is abundant cover is another method, the one which leopards and most of the other cat species use. But where open spaces are also available many prey species avoid thick cover, for over the generations those individuals which did not avoid it were likely to fall victim more often to the predators waiting there for them. To catch prey which live in open country the proto-lions probably took tentatively to hunting in groups; by doing so they improved the likelihood of each hunt being successful, mainly because they got second and perhaps third chances when a prey animal, fleeing from one pursuing cat, ran close to another unseen one.

A number of consequences soon follow from regularly hunting in groups. Each predator obviously gets less food for each kill made, because there are more hungry mouths wanting a share of the meat. Therefore, for it to be worthwhile for an individual proto-lion to hunt with others, either their hunting success must be improved, or they must kill larger prey animals, or both. Killing larger prey becomes possible once the proto-lions hunt together habitually. Several predators can more easily pull down and kill a large victim, and can do so with less risk of injury than to a solitary cat. If two or more lions are working together, for example, one may be able to wound the vulnerable rear end of a buffalo while the second is being kept at bay by the threat of the horns at the front. I saw a vivid example of the problems involved in hunting alone when a lioness faced a slightly lame wildebeest bull. Normally wildebeest run away from lions, but this one could not run fast enough. But he could defend himself, and indeed chased the lioness vigorously whenever she tried to approach or to move round behind him. Equally he could not limp away because she started to run up behind him whenever he set off. Had his weapons been situated at his rear instead of at his front end, he might have been able to retreat safely. As it was, after holding off the lone hunter for nearly an hour he stupidly committed suicide by sitting down, and the lioness seized him just before he could rise. If she had had a companion, the contest would have lasted no time at all.

Injury while tackling prey becomes not only less likely but also slightly less serious to a group hunter than to a solitary one, because a wounded individual may be able to feed from kills made by its companions until it recovers. I have often seen lions which were so seriously lame or injured that they could move only slowly; yet thanks to being able to sustain themselves on the food captured by other members of their pride, they survived and recovered. By contrast, I seldom saw seriously wounded leopards and cheetahs partly, I think, because they risk injury less and partly because once wounded they tend to die of starvation through their inability to hunt, as that lame cheetah nearly did.

Once proto-lions could regularly tackle larger prey, there would have been selective pressures on them to become larger themselves. The big herbivores living unpreyed upon in relatively open country would have provided a new food supply for them, and larger predators would be better able to make use of that opportunity. A single predator only catches prey somewhat smaller than itself, as I described for both leopards and cheetahs. A team of two or three predators can catch prey much more than two or three times as large so the group now has surplus food available to it, and can be composed of larger animals. This increased size would almost certainly be advantageous to a predator feeding habitually on prey much larger than itself, for it can then kill that prey with even less risk of injury.

Once the proto-lions had started out along this road towards greater size and group hunting, natural selection would have pushed them further along it. After all, larger prey have a higher vantage point than smaller animals from which to detect the approach of a predator; at the same time that predator was itself becoming larger and more difficult to conceal. Effectively this would be equivalent to the country becoming more open, and would force the proto-lions to develop more effective methods of social hunting such as by co-operating better. As I have said, much hunting by the large Serengeti cats is opportunistic: they wait until a chance to catch prey arises. It was pure chance that the lame wildebeest happened to limp near to where the lioness was resting. Since it is impossible to predict when such chances may occur, a predator which needs to hunt in groups needs also to live together in groups. There are likely to be a number of advantages in having permanent groups rather than loose temporary associations: the individuals probably benefit by knowing each others' hunting methods and temperaments. The most obvious way of forming a group of proto-lions would be for the young to remain together, perhaps with their mother, instead of dispersing independently. In this way the group is composed of individuals who are already familiar with one another, and who have a genetic interest in one another's well-being, an aspect I look at further in the next chapter.

Living in permanent social groups would bring further advantages to proto-lions, in addition to the ability to catch larger prey and to do so in more open habitats. A single lioness is no match for a pack of hyaenas, and I have seen them on occasions drive her from her kill and even force her to escape up a tree. A group of lions, though, can and does put hyaenas to flight. Thus the proto-lions' social living, together with their increasing size, would have enabled them to compete more effectively with the various other species of predators and scavengers. Among their rivals would be other groups of proto-lions too, and the larger and more organized groups would probably compete against them better. Sickness, like injury, would be less serious to the social proto-lions than to their solitary ancestors because the need to hunt independently would have disappeared; the individuals would have greater freedom of movement because they could leave their cubs protected by other group members.

These various advantages would all have accrued once proto-lions became social because of their new hunting technique. We should ask, therefore, why the other two cats in the same environment, the leopard and the cheetah, do not also forsake their solitary way of life so as to reap these benefits of social living. From what has been said already of their hunting, I think we can see the answer to these questions.

The cheetah had already diverged from the common cat ancestor long before lions and leopards separated, and had become specialized for very high speed, overtaking prey in open country with very little cover. The country has to be open, because obstacles such as trees hinder a large predator more than its small prey; for example, a small dog can get through a crowd quicker than a man can. Cheetahs' adaptation for speed means that they are relatively unarmed and delicate predators, so they can only take prey which are considerably smaller than themselves and unable to resist. The average cheetah victim supplies enough food for a single cheetah and her cubs, but it would not provide enough each among several adults. Thus, for it to be worthwhile for a cheetah to hunt its necessarily small prey with a companion, its success rate would have to be doubled; otherwise it would do better on its own. A cheetah's success rate is already quite

84 A wildebeest bull, slightly lame with a swollen left foreleg, finds itself facing a lioness which has managed to get within close range of him. He keeps her at bay with the threat of his horns and greater size

85 Whenever he starts to move away, however, she starts to creep rapidly up towards him

86 When she gets too close he charges at her, and she has to take quick evasive action

186

87 Deadlock – she cannot approach, and he cannot leave

88 Still watched by her potential victim, she rolls playfully on the ground

89 Eventually he sits down. She then gets quickly to her feet and runs round behind him . . .

90 . . . from where she manages to seize him before he can get up and charge her
91 She holds her victim by the throat, thus strangling and suffocating him

92 After a couple of minutes the wildebeest topples to the ground

93 The lioness holds the wildebeest's throat until he is dead, then laboriously drags him towards the shade, pausing for breath at intervals

high – nearly 50 per cent of its chases result in a kill – and so it would be hard put to achieve twice that success rate; in fact I doubt whether its hunting success would be improved at all, let alone doubled. The problem for a cheetah in open country is to approach within about thirty or forty yards of its prey undetected. If two cheetahs were trying to do this, it would be twice as likely that one of them would be detected; the prey then flees, straight, and because the detection distance in open country is so great, the prey would not be surrounded and would probably escape. In such open country the problems involved in surrounding prey without being seen are tremendous, and the distances the cheetahs would have to travel would be great. Every movement makes a cheetah liable to detection, either by the intended meal or by another prey animal which snorts an alarm call and thereby warns the target. Thus, because they have to hunt small prey and have to do it in open country, cheetahs could benefit little from hunting in groups. They have diverged along an evolutionary line which makes them unable to participate in the other, later, advantages of social living.

It seems that leopards have remained solitary for different reasons. Their ecological niche, as I described, is hunting small prey animals in thick cover. The problem with catching small animals in this habitat is that they can escape easily, as I saw them do, by flying, going up trees or down holes, or by dodging through or round bushes and other obstacles where a large pursuer cannot follow at speed. Thus the leopard has to be able to stalk to within a very short distance of its victims before rushing at them. Essentially it catches them before they can flee, rather than as they are fleeing. This is not easy. An alert dikdik, for example, is exceedingly difficult to stalk: its sensitive ears and nose are likely to detect the approach of a large predator, and probably twice as likely to detect the approach of two large predators. Thus a pair of leopards hunting together, using silent, stealthy approaches or ambushes, would probably not help one another appreciably; by analogy, cat-burglars also work on their own. If a victim were caught, each hunter would get only half as much food as if it had been alone and caught that prey animal. One might suppose that leopards could move along the evolutionary route which the proto-lions took and try to catch larger prey in more open country. But if they were to adopt this approach, in other words to start to evolve into proto-lions themselves, they would soon find themselves in ecological competition with the already adapted lions, who would be much better at being lions than evolving leopards would be. The larger cats would also be able to rob the leopards of much of their food, since the latter would no longer be able to carry their bigger prey up trees, the importance of which I have outlined. The social hunting cat niche has now been filled by lions and thus is no longer empty, as it was before, for a new large cat species to exploit.

It can be misleading to stress only the advantageous consequences of social living, for there can be disadvantages too. For example, if lions manage to catch only small prey animals many of their cubs may starve; on the other hand they produce larger litters than leopards, so a higher mortality is naturally to be expected. In areas where there are big populations of prey animals, such as in the Serengeti, lions live at a density about twice as high as leopards, and thus could be said to be twice as successful there. Yet the range of habitats which lions can use is not nearly as varied as those used by leopards; worldwide, leopards are far more numerous and, in that sense, more successful than lions. Both, though, may fairly be considered more successful than cheetahs, whose numbers are low everywhere and whose habitat requirements are narrow.

Other carnivore species have also become social. In the same environment, the Serengeti, are found also spotted hyaenas and wild dogs. Both live in permanent social groups, those of hyaenas being much less close-knit than those of the wild dogs. Both hunt in packs, hyaenas mainly at night and wild dogs mostly by day, and both hunt in the canid fashion of running their prey down by a long pursuit. (Dogs are chasers, while cats are stalkers, then sprinters.) Both hyaenas and wild dogs manage to kill prey considerably larger than themselves, and both do it in relatively open country, in the plains more than in the woodlands in the Serengeti. Spotted hyaenas are abundant and successful there, much more so than the solitary striped hyaena which feeds on a wide variety of small food items which it finds or scavenges. Wild dogs, on the other hand, like cheetahs, are surprisingly scarce for such apparently skilful hunters.

Jackals are abundant and versatile. They do most of their foraging alone but will often hunt gazelle fawns in pairs. If they do, they usually succeed because one can draw off the defending mother gazelle while the other kills her fawn; by contrast, one jackal alone usually does not manage to catch a healthy fawn protected by its mother. In northern Europe and America, the wolf is another carnivore which has become social, successful, large and capable of feeding on prey considerably larger than itself. And of course man has managed to do the same.

We should now consider what further selective pressures were likely to have operated on these proto-lions as they were gradually increasing in size, hunting in groups and killing larger prey in more open country. Lions' ancestors were probably spotted, judging by the spotting still to be found on the fur of present-day lion cubs and often still visible on the legs of adults. Presumably their more uniform coat was an adaptation to the more uniform colourings characteristic of open country where there are not so many patches of dappled shade, nor variegated leaves, nor so many potential prey species with colour vision, all factors which presumably favour the leopard's beautiful spotted coat colouring. Lions' pale fur is also a better reflector of heat than the leopard's darker average colour. This would probably have helped the proto-lions because they would have been gradually becoming more diurnal, and living in an open habitat where less shade was available; their greater size would also have contributed to the problems which large tropical animals face in keeping cool. The unique tail tuft may well have developed at about this time, probably as a fly whisk, and more necessary for a cat which has to stay out in the open during the day; its conspicuous black colour could aid its use as a signal to other members of the social group.

We can continue with the probable trends in lions' evolution. As the proto-lions were becoming larger and needing more food, a group of them would obviously require a larger area than did their smaller solitary ancestor. My lions' territories were several times the size of those of my leopards, although not as much larger as was the weight of the lions occupying them. It takes more energy to defend a large territory than a small one because there is much further to travel. Lions do less scent-marking of their territory than leopards. Instead, perhaps, they have developed the roar, a sound which carries much further than the calls of any other cat species. A loud noise becomes more necessary as the area to be defended becomes larger, and as there are more companions to be kept in touch with and informed of one another's whereabouts. In all this I do not mean to imply that one characteristic evolved first and was later followed by another: it is more likely that several developed gradually together, although some were consequent upon others.

Competition between the males would soon have increased. A group of proto-lions consisting of one or more adult females and grown-up

8   Two lionesses with cubs look intently towards where they suspect there is prey

9   Lions playing with a zebra carcass before starting to feed on it

10 A wildebeest faces a lioness

11 A hungry lioness and several starving cubs struggle desperately over the remains of a small kill

12   Two lionesses groom the head of a cub which has got filthy while feeding

13   A gathering group of vultures waits for a cheetah family to leave the remains of its kill

14   Lions watch for prey at sunset

offspring, and occupying a territory where food was to be found throughout the year, would be a unit much sought after by a male. Owning one, he would be able to mate with several females and so produce a large number of young. Since probably as many males as females were born, some would not have a resident breeding group to attach themselves to. They would be unable to breed unless they could drive out a male already attached, and since he would be unlikely to go voluntarily, fighting would be necessary. There are two obvious ways of improving your chances in a fight: by being bigger and stronger than your opponent (which I shall deal with in a moment), and by having a companion also fighting on your side. Coalitions of two or more males would be favoured by natural selection. Although partnership involves sharing the prize, that prize lasts for longer: I have already described how having companions lengthens the males' tenure of a pride of lionesses. It would not be difficult for this kind of co-operation to arise and develop in a species which is already dependent on co-operation for catching prey, and in which the young have a long growing-up period together. Thus selection would favour tolerance and co-operation among the members of a coalition, and competition between different male groups, and this we see in modern lions.

The females no doubt would have exercised some choice over which males were attached to their group and with whom they mated. We would expect them to have preferred to mate with males who were fit and who were not related to them. In this way the females would ensure that their own offspring were more likely to be both fit and free of the deficiencies which inbred animals often show. The adult males attached to the group would gain by forcing out any young males which had grown up in the group, because the younger animals might become rivals later and, in any case, would consume food which would otherwise feed the adult males and their offspring. The adult males would also assist the females in keeping intruders of both sexes out of the group's territory, and thus the females gain some advantages from their attached males.

On the other hand, a group of female proto-lions feeding on large kills is liable to be parasitized by males for food. In all cats the males are larger and stronger than females, and therefore potentially capable of stealing their food. But if the female is a solitary cat feeding on small prey animals it is difficult for a male to make a regular living by stealing her kills, because she can consume them so quickly. Even if she did not and he was able to rob her of them, she would find it difficult alone to catch enough food to support herself, her cubs and a male going in for full-time plundering. On the other hand, a group of proto-lions can be regularly robbed, partly because the kills are larger, but also because the burden of providing food for a couple of food-parasitic males is distributed over several females. Each female has in effect to support only a portion of a male. The females may not be particularly willing to share their kills, but the males have the important advantage of size and strength. When food is normally plentiful it is probably not worthwhile for the females to risk a fight to try to prevent males feeding from their kill; their safer options are to go and catch another one or to feed on the remains.

Once they have been freed from the necessity of catching their own food, the males are affected by other selective pressures over the generations. They no longer need to be adapted to hunting. It seems that whereas the females, as in other cat species, are still primarily hunting animals, evolution has converted male lions into animals better adapted for fighting. The males, from their own point of view, need to be good at winning possession of a pride from other males, and at beating off subsequent challengers. I think that both their greater size and, particularly, their mane are examples of adaptations for doing so. Other things being equal, larger animals tend to be better at winning fights than smaller ones, as the boxing world well knows. Thus we might expect that male lions would be continuously increasing in size in the course of evolution. On the other hand, larger animals require more food and are less agile than small ones, so there is a top limit to how large they can become before the net advantages of size disappear. In most animals, many conflicts are settled without any blows being struck, when one animal, perhaps a smaller one, perceives that it is likely to be the loser if a fight should develop. Therefore a lion which can in effect cheat by *appearing* extra large without actually *being* extra large would do well at intimidating potential opponents yet would not suffer the other disadvantages of large size. The mane of a male lion is ideally suited to this purpose: like a padded military uniform, it makes the wearer look much larger and thus more likely to win a fight, and so his opponents are more inclined to give way without starting one. No doubt the mane has other functions too: it probably protects its owner's neck against claw wounds in fights, and it may also act as a conspicuous signal. Often the apparently huge head and shoulders of a male meant that I could spot him far away, where a female would be too small to see; I presume that intruding lions with eyes like mine would similarly become aware of his presence sooner and would stay clear of him. The mane almost certainly hampers the male if he does hunt, because it makes it more difficult for him to be inconspicuous when stalking towards prey animals – it is not hard to detect a walking haystack! This does not matter to the adult males in possession of a pride, because they seldom need to catch their own food. When subadult males are still nomadic they must be able to hunt, but their manes are still small at that stage; also they can get a larger proportion of their food by scavenging naturally dead carcasses or the kills of smaller predators. One way in which the males' size and strength may help them and the pride is in bringing down extra large prey such as adult buffaloes, but on the whole the males' contribution to a lion pride's food budget is strongly negative: they take much more than they give.

Given that males have been selected particularly as fighting animals, the lack of competition among the pride males for an oestrous female is most striking, especially when compared with the many species where the males fight vigorously for any receptive female. We would expect each male to make some effort to propagate his own genes rather than just sit by while someone else does so. I think that part of the reason for the males' lack of effort is that any mating is most unlikely to produce surviving offspring. How unlikely? We can calculate on the basis of the information in Chapter 4. If in an oestrous period lions mate on average every fifteen minutes for three days, if four out of five of those oestrous periods do not result in litters of cubs being born, if the average litter size is two or three cubs, and if three out of four of those cubs die, then well over two thousand matings are needed for each cub which is successfully reared to the next generation. With so low a likelihood of ultimate success, it is small wonder that natural selection has not made companion males fight for the privilege of fathering a fraction of a thousandth of a cub, for fighting would involve considerable risks of injury to the lions, equipped with weapons as they are. Also to some extent, of course, the competition for an oestrous female is so slight because some of it has already taken place during two earlier stages. First, there has already been severe competition between rival male groups for possession of the pride containing the female in question; and second, because the mating male got possession of the oestrous female before his companions did, he is very temporarily dominant while he is with her, as I described, by a kind of gentlemen's agreement about ownership. But as we know in our own species, gentlemen's agreements are more lasting when the stakes are low.

Why are the stakes so low? Why is lions' reproduction apparently so inefficient? Why are so many copulations necessary for a lion pregnancy, when most species manage with many fewer? Part of the answer lies I think in the relaxation of the selective pressures which normally favour reproductive efficiency; in other words, it does not matter so much if lions mate unduly often. There are probably three reasons why it does not matter. First, lions do not have a birth season: they may produce their cubs at any time of the year, so a failure to become pregnant after an oestrous period does not mean that a whole year's reproduction has been lost, merely that it has been delayed by a few weeks. Second, lions usually have plenty of spare time – after all, as I had ample time to observe, they spend three-quarters of their lives inactive – and food is usually plentiful. If they squander some of their time and energy on fruitless mating they do not lose anything which is in short supply. And third, adult lions run no risk of being preyed upon, so the noise and conspicuousness of frequent mating does not matter as it would to a smaller animal which made itself so conspicuous and thus vulnerable to predators quite so often. The same three reasons might apply in the case of humans.

We have seen why we should not expect reproduction in lions to be highly efficient, but certainly we would not predict that it would be so strikingly *in*efficient. Lionesses often come into oestrus and mate, but do not produce cubs as a result. Possibly mating has acquired functions which are social rather than solely procreational, such as strengthening the social bonds between a male and a female, as has been suggested in many species including our own. I must confess that I doubt whether this is important in lions. The readiness with which an oestrous lion will mate with a stranger and her apparent lack of discrimination among her pride males both imply that individual social bonds between the sexes are neither strong, nor strengthened by mating between those individuals. Nor, I think, being highly anthropomorphic for a moment, do male lions actually enjoy the sexual process much, although judging by their behaviour afterwards I think females might. However, this is not of great relevance to my argument.

I think it is useful to look at the logical consequences of lions' mating inefficiency. I assume that a male cannot tell whether a female will or will not conceive as a result of his mating with her; if he could I would expect to observe two different kinds of mating pattern – either social or productive. One consequence, as we have seen, is that each copulation is in a sense of very little genetical 'value' to a male: on average it results in his producing only a minute fraction of a cub, too small to be worth the risk of fighting his companions for. And precisely this – preventing their pride males from fighting one another – may be one of the reasons why the lionesses have evolved their readiness to mate so often and unavailingly: their 'inefficiency' may be a peace-keeping adaptation.

How does it help the lionesses if their pride males do not fight each other? If the latter battle with and injure one another, they may be weakened by their wounds or reduced in number by deaths. If this happens, they will soon be driven out as the pride is taken over by a new group of males. Such a takeover, as we have seen, is a considerable setback to the females, for their reproduction is delayed and some of their cubs are killed by the newcomers. We would expect natural selection to have favoured the evolution of any methods by which the lionesses can delay or mitigate such setbacks, even if they cannot prevent them. One such method is by discouraging the resident male lions from fighting, therefore delaying the takeover of the pride and so improving their cubs' chances of survival. And it is done by giving them less to fight for.

We have come a long way from the lion ancestor at the start of this chapter, and have seen how various new selective pressures can arise once lions set off on the road towards social living. In the next chapter we see further complex selective pressures operating in different ways on different *individuals* in the lion population.

10 · Lions' genes

The selective pressures I have mentioned so far have been mainly the ones which I presume to have operated in the past and to have made lions what they are today. But natural selection never stops, and in this chapter I want to consider some of the selective pressures operating on lions now. Given the social system I have observed and described, which lions within it leave more descendants than others, and why?

THE REPRODUCTION RACE

It is important to consider the evolution of lions, as of other animals, at the level of the individual rather than of the species as a whole. Charles Darwin described clearly the way in which in nature there is a 'struggle for survival': some individuals in a species are better adapted to their environment than others, and so are more likely to survive and to pass on to succeeding generations the genes which made them better adapted. The 'struggle' does not imply conscious competition, but the effects of selection make it appear as though a struggle has taken place. Only live lions can produce offspring, of course, so any which do not survive do not contribute any of their genes to the next generation. However, there is a second stage to this struggle. Some lions produce and rear more cubs than others, and therefore in just the same way any genes which helped to make them produce more will get passed on to those offspring. Consequently we expect a lion to contain genes which make him or her both good at surviving and good at producing many surviving lion cubs.

To be good at surviving, a lion must have all the characteristics I have described earlier in this book – strength, skill at hunting, ability to overcome diseases and wounds, and so on. If a lioness is better than others at all this, she probably produces more cubs, and so passes on more of the genes which make her better, and these make the next generation better too. The species as a whole 'benefits' by being improved in this way through the natural selection race, the race to leave most descendants. But there are more ways of winning a race than just by being a fast runner. For example, you can start sooner than your rivals, you can hamper them in their running, and you might persuade or bully another runner to push you along faster still or to help you hinder the others. If the winners of uncontrolled races like these passed on their methods to the next generations of runners and the losers did not, we would expect to see developing some very complicated strategies for winning races, such as coalitions and elaborate methods for eliminating the other competitors. After a while, the kind of person who tended to win most races would not necessarily be just the slim swift type – he would combine the characteristics of the general, the genius, the boxer, and the man with many friends and relations. He would probably be quite a good runner too, but not as fast as if he had been selected for running speed alone. The 'species' of runner would not have benefited. Other selective pressures would have come into play, and what kind of pressures depend on what kind of race it is, what rules, what terrain, and who else is competing.

We can see some obvious analogies with lions. I have described the fighting between rival male groups, for example, the coalitions of males against those rival groups, and the co-operative life of a pride which enables all the lionesses in it to improve their chances of catching prey or rearing young. All are strategies by which particular lions pass on more of their genes to future generations than if they did not use these strategies. Male lions are, in effect, competing in a different race from the females, and thus the characteristics they need to do well in it are different. Fighting ability, for example, is more important for males than for females, and the large size and mane of the males reflect this importance.

There are other ways in which a group of male lions competes in the reproduction race against other males. When new males have managed to take possession of a pride, they are liable to kill at least some of that pride's cubs. Why do they do so, and what effects does it have? In immediate terms, a new male kills those cubs probably because they are strangers who smell unfamiliar to him. He does not do so because he

94 A male lion who has recently taken over a pride carries in his mouth a four-month-old cub he has killed. By this infanticide, he manages to produce more of his own offspring

just cannot help pouncing on small animals, since except in the first few months of his tenure of a pride a male does not harm the cubs in it, and indeed is extremely tolerant towards them.

However, we can see that a male who does kill cubs when he and his companions take over a pride will on average leave more offspring than males who do not. The pride which he takes over is most unlikely to be the pride in which he was born; therefore a new male is not closely related to the cubs he kills, and so he has no genetic 'interest' in their welfare. On the other hand, he is programmed to produce as many cubs of his own as possible. I showed that if a lioness's cubs die she generally produces another litter about nine months later, whereas if her cubs were to survive she would not give birth again until those cubs were about two years old. In either case, the new male will be the father of this next litter, and so if he kills existing cubs which are not his own, he becomes a father sooner. Thus he will father more cubs during his ownership of the pride; they will survive better in the absence of the older cubs of his predecessor; and they will be older when he in turn is eventually expelled, and so they will be less subject to mortality at the teeth of his successor. The male's period of tenure is short, so the extra proportion of cubs he produces by this behaviour is significant. There have been strong selective pressures on male lions to do things (such as killing cubs) which increase the number of offspring they produce; and these selective pressures are all the stronger because their successors will use similar tactics. Thus cub-killing begets further cub-killing, and the male who indulges in it at the moment when he takes over a pride leaves more descendants than a male who does not. These descendants will be likely to carry inside them whatever genes made their ancestor kill cubs, and in time this behaviour will become universal among male lions, because it is to the 'advantage' of a male to do it. Note that to say that a certain piece of behaviour is 'advantageous' to, or 'benefits', a lion is a shorthand way of saying that one who exhibits that behaviour will on average leave more offspring than another lion who does not. Note too that the lion is of course completely unconscious of these selective pressures; he merely does what male lions have been selected to do over the generations, and considerations of right or wrong similarly do not occur to trouble him.

Clearly it is not to the advantage of a lioness to have her cubs killed, and so we should consider why she has not evolved any good strategy to counter the behaviour of the new males. There are considerable practical problems facing her. A female with small cubs tends to avoid newly arrived males, but the latter are much more mobile than her cubs, so this strategy cannot be completely effective. She cannot defend her cubs all the time if she is to catch food for them: it is no good guarding her cubs if in consequence they die of starvation instead of by violence. Guarding is also a difficult thing to do if there are two males near her. She can threaten one if he comes very close, as I have seen her do, but she cannot leave her cubs to attack him; and once he has grabbed a cub it is dead instantly so then attacking him is not worth while because it is too late. A lioness is considerably smaller than a male, and so she would come off worse in a fight with him, which doubtless discourages her from too vigorous a defence of her young. In any case it may not be worth it, because young cubs are relatively expendable even to their mother: they are minute compared with her, have taken little time or energy to produce, and can be replaced quickly and many times over in the course of a lioness's lifetime. Most of them will probably die anyway, of one cause or another. They do not merit as much effort or risk by their mother on their behalf as they would if, like human or elephant infants, they represented a considerable investment

201

of parental time and energy. Again, the lioness is not conscious of such considerations. Over the generations, lionesses who tried too hard to defend their cubs will have produced fewer surviving offspring in their lifetime than lionesses who did not, and thus natural selection has weighed up these points. As a result, and in view of the great practical difficulties involved, it is not surprising that lionesses have not evolved any really effective defence method. Nonetheless they would do better, in the sense that they would leave more offspring, if their cubs were not killed by new males; we see clearly a conflict of advantages between the two sexes.

It is obvious that killing cubs does not benefit the lion species as a whole. There is no reason why it should, for natural selection operates at the level of the individuals within the species. Those individual lions who leave more surviving offspring contribute more genes to future generations, and if those genes include some which do not benefit the species but help only some of the individuals within it, those genes will still be selected for and will proliferate. The harm to the species is also fairly small: even with this mortality, the prides I observed managed to rear more than enough lion cubs to replace adult losses; there were a surplus who were expelled, and so presumably became nomadic and did not reproduce effectively. Cub-killing by males is a mildly detrimental by-product of the lions' elaborate social system, and a small price to pay for the success lions have achieved through becoming social. It is also, I think, now an entirely understandable piece of behaviour, although at first sight it might be considered to be maladaptive or aberrant.

Let us also consider some of the selective pressures operating on other aspects of lions' reproduction. When new males take over a pride there is likely to be a period of several months when no litters are born to females in that pride. During the first three months of that time we would have expected births by females who had been made pregnant by the previous males, yet this does not happen. Why not? It is possible that the previous males were becoming less fertile, although there are no signs of this. It seems more probable either that the females detected the imminent departure of their pride males and that this prevented them from conceiving, or else that they were in fact pregnant but aborted their foetuses because of the presence or smell of the newly arrived males. It is clearly to the advantage of the new males not to have those cubs born, for that would delay the production of their own young. It is less easy to see how the females benefit by not producing young, so why should they have evolved a readiness to respond in this way? The answer is probably that the new males would be likely to kill any cubs the females did produce, and that the lionesses can therefore save themselves the waste of effort needed to produce them. Here again, what is to the advantage of the new males conflicts with the 'interests' of the females, but this time the result is an adaptation by the females, reducing the harm done to their interests by this conflict. In many respects, the effect of new males in causing females to abort their predecessors' offspring is equivalent to killing those offspring when born: both are aspects of the intense competition between groups of male lions, and both are ways in which the newcomers increase their own reproductive output at the expense of their rival predecessors.

I found in the Serengeti that lionesses tend to synchronize birth with other lionesses in the same pride, with the result that cubs were often in batches of the same age. What mechanisms and what selective pressures make them do this? Pheromones or scent signals, either among the females or from males to females, may be important as the mechanism for producing a rough synchrony of conceptions, but we don't yet know how it works at all. Why the females have evolved a readiness to respond in this way is also worth thinking about. There seem to be two main reasons. First, a lioness's cubs are more likely to survive through infancy if they are born in synchrony, probably because they can suckle from other lactating females. Later they can associate with other cubs of similar size, who are neither larger and liable to plunder them of food, nor smaller and liable to delay their progress by being much weaker. Second, especially for males, it helps lions as adults to have companions. If a female is recruited into her pride she has companions anyway, but if she is expelled she probably does much better to have one or more female companions with whom she leads her nomadic life, and with whom she just might be able to found a new pride. A group of lions has less difficulty in making kills or displacing hyaenas or other lions from carcasses than does a single one. For a male there is an extra and very important value in having two or more companions, namely that they enable him to retain possession of a pride for much longer than he could either alone or with one brother. For a long and successful reproductive life a male lion needs to have at least two other male companions with whom to hold joint ownership of a pride for several years. But most litters contain no more than four cubs; on average only half of these are male, and fewer than half of those are likely to reach adulthood. If a lioness in a pride produces a litter when no other lioness does, any surviving male cub will probably be on his own when the time comes for him to be expelled from his pride. If, on the other hand, she gives birth at the same time as other lionesses, her subadult son is much more likely to be able to leave in the company of other subadults and so embark on a much more successful reproductive life. Thus a lioness who gives birth in synchrony with others improves the survival chances of her cubs of both sexes, and further increases the number of grandchildren she will have through her sons.

RELATEDNESS AND KIN SELECTION

We have seen that the lionesses in a pride were all born in that pride, and that strange females are not permitted to join. Lion prides probably last for many generations, as old females die and are replaced by young ones who are their daughters, grand-daughters, nieces and so on. Thus all the females in a pride are genetically related to one another. Some will be close relatives such as sisters, mothers and daughters, while others will be half-sisters or more distant aunts and cousins. Obviously if all the lionesses are genetically related to one another, all their cubs will also be related both to all the lionesses in the pride and to one another. Therefore two or three males leaving their pride together will also be related to one another; they stay together during their nomadic years, and it is still as a group that a couple of years later they take over a different pride as the breeding males there. Thus the adult males in a pride are inter-related, and so are the females. But the males are not closely related, if at all, to the females.

If the males, for example, are related to one another, how closely are they related? Two young males leaving a pride together will sometimes be litter-mates and so presumably full brothers. On the other hand, because a lioness may mate with more than one male during her oestrous period, it is possible that the animals in one litter could be fathered by different males; if so, since those fathers are probably related to one another, their offspring would be extra-close half brothers. Male companions may often be from different litters produced synchronously by different mothers; in this case they may or may not share the same father, and their mothers may be closely or distantly related to one another. Thus companion males could be brothers or they could be fairly distant cousins. By making certain assumptions

204

about typical prides, I have been able to calculate that on average they will usually be about as closely related as half-brothers are to one another; by contrast, any two lionesses in a pride will on average be about as inter-related as first cousins. In each case this is the average figure of what is most likely, the average being made up of a range of relatednesses, some closer such as sisters and some more distant such as first cousins once removed. These differing degrees of relatedness among the various animals in a pride provide the basis for much of the lions' social organization and behaviour – the cohesiveness and co-operation among females and among males, but the 'apartness' of the males from the females.

95 A six-week-old cub with another of about five months. Note the marked dark spots on the forehead of the small cub

I said earlier in this chapter that natural selection operates at the level of individuals, but what each individual animal – whether lion, lamb, man or mouse – actually passes on to its offspring are some of its own genes, or rather, a random collection of half of its innumerable genes. These, found in the cell nuclei of every animal, are the units of genetic material which determine much of the development, form and behaviour of that animal. Each animal itself received half of its genes from one of its parents and half from the other. Then as it produces sperms or eggs it in effect randomly reshuffles those genes, half of which go into each sperm or egg. When an egg is fertilized, the arriving sperm from another animal brings more genes to provide the full complement to make another new individual. Because there are a vast number of genes, each animal has a unique combination of them, and so every individual is different. But because half of their genes were derived from each parent, an offspring usually bears a resemblance to its parent, reflecting the 50 per cent of genes which on average they have in common. Similarly, two brothers or sisters from the same pair of parents also resemble one another because they too share, on average, 50 per cent of their genes with one another, each having a different random assortment of half of each parents' genes. More distant relatives are likely to share a lower proportion of genes with one another. For example, a mother passes on half of her genes to her daughter, who in turn passes on half of them to her own offspring; therefore, a grandmother, on average, shares only a quarter of her genes with her grandchildren. Similarly two half-brothers, or an aunt and her niece, are also likely to have a quarter of their genes in common, while first counsins share only around an eighth. We all know that cousins generally look less alike than brothers but often show some resemblances.

Natural selection is the process whereby some genes become commoner and some more scarce in an animal species. Suppose, for example, that a lion has among her genes a new one which makes her better at catching prey. As a result she will manage to rear more cubs; roughly half of these cubs will carry this beneficial gene, and they in turn will do better at catching food and rearing cubs than other lions without the gene. Eventually, after many generations, all the lions in the population will be carriers of this helpful gene. Through natural selection the lion species will have become more efficient, as a result of the new gene managing to outcompete its rival genes by making the animals which carry it able to produce more offspring and therefore more replicas of itself.

For lion cubs to survive, they must be looked after. A lioness rears her cubs because she has the genes which make her behave in the appropriate way. If she had instead a gene which made her behave inadequately, she would leave no offspring, and so her inappropriate gene would not be replicated and propagated in future generations. Suppose, on the other hand, that she had a gene which made her willing to rear her dead sister's cubs as well as her own, provided that she had spare time and milk. That gene would be found in roughly half of her own offspring and would be propagated through them; but there would also have been a 50 per cent chance that the same gene would have been in her dead sister and therefore a 25 per cent chance that it would be in any one of that sister's cubs. If she helps those cubs to survive, this relation-helping gene would be propagated in greater numbers than a rival gene responsible for helping only her own offspring, and so eventually outcompete the latter and spread through the lion population.

Because the offspring of an animal's close relatives bear a proportion of its own genes, those offspring have in a sense a genetic 'value' to it in the same way that its own offspring have. Their value is less than the value of its own offspring because they have fewer genes in common, but they have a value nonetheless. Rearing relatives' children is a form of reproduction just like rearing one's own, albeit a more diluted form: both carry a proportion of one's own genes into subsequent generations, one's own children bearing twice as many as one's brother's children and eight times as many as one's cousin's children. My five nephews and nieces are carrying into the next generation as many of my genes as if I had produced two-and-a-half children of my own.

Animals are not usually altruistic. They do not often help one another unless their own self-interest is also served. The obvious exception is, of course, helping offspring, who may be lavishly supplied with food and care. Another exception is helping the mate, which is really another indirect way of helping the offspring. A further, less common exception is helping other close relatives who, like offspring, share a proportion of the helper's genes. Not all animals help their relatives, often because the latter are far away, or unknown, or incapable of being helped. A wildebeest cow, for example, probably does not know who her sister is, even if she ever met her, and it would be difficult for them to help one another in their feeding. Most lions, on the other hand, spend their whole lives among their relations, there are more ways in which they can help them, and in many of these they also help themselves. In fact lions' social behaviour revolves around the complicated balance of self-interest and the interests of other pride members of different degrees of relatedness. The lions are, of course, not conscious of this balance, nor of what being related means. They just do whatever their genes make, encourage or allow them to do. Natural selection does the weighing, as it favours successful genes – those which encourage behaviour patterns which cause more of those genes to be transmitted to the next generation of lions.

Lions co-operate in many ways. A striking one is in their group hunting. In most communal hunts, all the animals in the group benefit from co-operating because the hunt is more likely to be successful, so it is easy to see how natural selection favours group hunting. The same applies to the co-operation among adult males when fighting against a rival group of males, for all the members of the winning group benefit from their victory. Grooming by one lion of the head and neck of a companion no doubt helps to keep the latter free of dirt and parasites; the groomed animal often reciprocates and licks the groomer, and thus both lions benefit. Lionesses tend to be close to and to groom the other females and cubs to whom they are related, rather than the males to whom they are not.

Lions also co-operate in rearing their young, and in particular a lioness will allow the cubs of other females in her pride to suckle from her. This is unusual in mammals. A wildebeest, for example, even one whose own calf has died, will not allow any of the innumerable, pathetic, lost, and so doomed, calves around to suckle from her; it is exceedingly unlikely that such a calf would be related to the adult wildebeest, and genes for helping non-relatives tend to be unsuccessful ones. By contrast, a lion cub suckling from a lioness who is not its mother is being helped by a relative. On average, as I have calculated, the various adult females would be somewhat more closely related than first cousins and so probably they share about one-seventh of their genes. A lioness, therefore, has a small but definite genetic interest in the well-being of her companions' offspring as well as of her own: more of her own genes reach future generations if her companions' cubs survive, and by allowing those cubs to suckle from her she helps them to survive. Her own cubs also benefit by the survival of those other cubs, particularly any young males who will later benefit from having companions by achieving a more successful reproductive life. Thus by allowing other cubs to suckle, a lioness helps both her relatives and her own offspring: it is small wonder in this case that such unusually altruistic behaviour has evolved in lions.

208

96 A male lion is tolerant towards cubs which might be his own or his companions' offspring. The two cubs on the left have been using him as a sunshade, and the cub on the right has been clambering over him in play; tiring of this, he is moving away

Lions are not altruistic in everything, nor towards every other lion. They are almost always hostile towards strangers, for example; and at kills, especially when food is in short supply, there is often quite a lot of squabbling as each individual tries to get as large a share as it can. On the other hand, lions in a pride do not organize themselves into a hierarchy where the unfortunate individual at the bottom is displaced or robbed by those above it. No lion has to avoid another member of the pride. This is probably a reflection of the fact that most animals in the pride are related, and so every individual has a genetic interest in the health and well-being of all the others.

I have already referred to the lack of competition among male lions for an oestrous female, and outlined several good evolutionary reasons why a male lion does better if he does not fight with his companions for the right to mate with a lioness and so propagate his genes. Among these reasons are the risks of being seriously injured and consequently ousted from his pride, and the probability that the mating would not result in cubs in any case. A further reason is that some of his genes are being passed on anyway: any cub which is fathered by his companion bears a number of them. If his companion is on average his half-brother, as I have calculated, he shares a quarter of his own genes. Therefore each of that companion's cubs carries about one-eighth of his genes, whereas his own cubs would have carried one half. Letting his companion mate instead can be looked on as a form of 'diluted reproduction by proxy', and although less effective at propagating his own genes than if he himself mated, it nevertheless contributes somewhat towards spreading his genes in future generations – and that is what an individual animal has been selected to do by one means or another. Whereas in most species this is done almost entirely by his own reproducing, in lions, with a large number of relatives around, a proportion of it is done by helping those relatives to reproduce too.

I had better stress yet again that none of these complexities I have discussed ever occurs to a lion. His decisions are largely made for him by the genes which made him into a lion and so make him behave like a lion. Natural selection has determined what kind of genes those are, by weighing up the net results of different strategies – to fight or not to fight, for example – and favouring those strategies which result in most genes in later generations. Nor of course are these selective pressures in any way visible to an observer watching a lion pride going about its business. I merely see one lioness letting another's cub suckle from her; I cannot *observe* what effect this has on how many of her genes will be in the lions my great-grandchildren will watch if they are fortunate enough.

11 · Lions and other animals

Other lions are, without doubt, the most significant animals in a lion's environment: I have described some of the ways in which lions interact with one another, and how this influences and is influenced by their social organization. Many other species are obviously important too, and here I want to discuss the ways in which lions interact with a variety of those other species, which I group into the four main categories of food, rivals, nuisances and man.

PREY SPECIES

Lions of course have profound, indeed usually fatal, effects on some individuals of the prey species on which they feed. In addition lion predation may limit the population sizes of those species, and it influences the way in which they evolve. I shall consider in turn each of these three kinds of interaction: with prey individuals, with prey populations and with prey species in the course of their evolution.

The main method of defence by most prey species is not to let a lion come close, which involves being thoroughly alert, looking up at frequent intervals, keeping an eye on companions and avoiding places where a lion is likely to be hidden. Topis, for example, often stand on termite mounds, from where they can get a good view of the country around. If the lion is not concealed, however, prey species are fairly unconcerned about it. I have often seen zebras, wildebeest and gazelles grazing within a hundred yards of a group of lions resting under trees in plain view of them, and taking remarkably little interest in their would-be consumers. I think the reason for their unconcern is not, as is often stated, that they can see that the lions are not hunting, for after all, lions are largely opportunistic hunters – but rather it is that (except at extremely close range) the lion you can see is not a danger to you. In open country, a visible lion at a hundred yards has not a hope of catching a healthy alert antelope, and both seem to know it. A walking lion evokes a little more interest, but not much greater avoidance.

However, suppose a wildebeest were to look up and see a lioness ten yards away and rushing at him. He would turn and run away, and probably get caught and killed. We might have expected him to defend himself with his powerful horns, which when backed up by his three-and-a-half hundredweight are formidable weapons: he does not use them, but runs instead. His horns, like the weapons on most other antelopes, are used for fighting other members of his own species, not for deterring predators. They can be used for this latter purpose, as I saw when a lame wildebeest faced and held off a single lioness for almost an hour, but this is exceedingly rare; wildebeest almost invariably flee, and probably with quite good reason. A lion is likely to be accompanied by one or more others who would together easily overcome the wildebeest's defence. Almost always the less hopeless chance is to accelerate fast and hope. A zebra can kick effectively with its hind legs while still running fast, but most escaping antelopes cannot use their main weapons – their horns – against a pursuer chasing them.

Even when it has been caught by lions, a prey animal rarely defends itself. It is probably in a state of considerable shock at first, from which it does not have time to recover before it is killed. It is difficult for it to do much when it has been brought down: it might hurt one or two of its attackers, but would be most unlikely to escape with its life. But unless animals which had been brought down did quite often manage to escape and survive, there is no way in which natural selection could favour the evolution of heroic but ineffectual defence at this stage.

Some animals come into the category of Invulnerables. The two main ones in this class in the Serengeti are elephants and rhinos. Although the small young of both these species are just occasionally killed by lions if not properly guarded in the usual way, the adults are effectively immune from predation, protected by their vast size and powerful pointed tusks or horns. On one occasion I watched an adult rhino tramp steadily right through the middle of a scattered pride of lions, virtually ignoring their presence. One or two of the lions directly in its path moved out of its way as it came close, but the rest scarcely budged, either towards or away from it. I got the impression that all the

97 One of the Semi-Invulnerables: an old bull buffalo. His massive horns and size protect him against all lions except determined and skilful groups. Note his horn bosses pitted with age, and his tattered ears

animals of both species knew that the rhino was not potential lion food. Another time I saw two lionesses and their cubs move quickly away into cover as a group of five bull elephants approached.

Adult buffaloes and giraffes I would classify as Semi-Invulnerables: they occasionally, though rarely, fall victim to lions. Both are far larger than any predator, and both can defend themselves, giraffes by kicking with their huge hooves, buffaloes by charging and jabbing with their immense horns. As a result, lions molest them only with care. Giraffes avoid lions more than buffaloes do. It is not rare for lions to be chased or treed by one or more buffaloes; indeed the latter I considered to be the most likely source of possible trouble for an immobilized lion, which I would therefore guard until it had recovered enough to avoid them. On the whole, however, buffaloes keep clear of lions – or try to. A number of adults of both species of Semi-Invulnerables are killed, and I do not know under what circumstances they became vulnerable. Giraffes probably put themselves most at risk when they splay out their legs wide apart and lower their neck in order to drink; in that posture they can neither see far nor stand up quickly to run or defend themselves. However, the few killed adult giraffes I found in the Serengeti were not near water; they might have been caught when sitting down, which they occasionally do.

The calves of these two species quite often become lion food, despite the protection of the adults. I was told of a young giraffe which was pulled down by a lioness who was subsequently driven off it by an adult female giraffe; although the calf got up and escaped, it was very badly wounded and had to be destroyed. That was the only time I heard of a giraffe chasing or attacking a lion. Buffaloes do so more often, and more vigorously in defence of a small calf. At dawn one morning I found a lion pride scattered on the tops of a collection of five small kopjes. This was unusual so early in the day, and the cause of it was the presence of a group of fifteen buffaloes below them; and the reason for their presence was that the male lion of the pride had under his paws a very small buffalo calf, alive and undamaged but bleating pathetically whenever the lion moved. At each bleat the buffaloes below milled about and snorted, apparently making the lion somewhat uneasy, and for over two hours until the buffaloes departed he made no attempt to start feeding.

Most other smaller species cannot and do not attack lions, nor do they defend themselves. However, there are a few exceptions. One is the ratel, or honey-badger, a small black-and-white badger-like animal with a ferocious temperament; it has the reputation of fearlessly attacking any animal which tries to molest it, biting and hanging on to its opponent. Another protected animal is the porcupine; its rattling quills provide an effective deterrent against the attentions of most lions in the Serengeti, who have never needed to learn the difficult technique of killing porcupines without feeling like a pincushion afterwards. A different kind of protection is achieved by the tortoises, which grow up to about eighteen inches in length. I have watched a group of lions trying to bite into the shell of a tortoise of about half that size, without success, but I have also found pieces of the shell of a smaller tortoise in a lion dropping, so the defence is probably not very good until the tortoise is fairly old. However, their shells are superbly camouflaged, and I doubt whether lions see or eat tortoises at all often. I never saw lions

214

encounter a poisonous snake, which I think they would avoid; I did however find a large python which had been killed by a lion but scarcely eaten.

The effects that lions have on the population of their prey are difficult to measure. Clearly, to some extent they must reduce it – each successful hunt makes the prey population contain one member less – but on the other hand the numbers which lions can take may be negligible compared with the numbers of live prey animals there are. Suppose for the moment that the 2000 lions in the Serengeti area were each to feed only on wildebeest, of which they ate 20 in a year (and these are maximum figures). Lions could not account for more than 40,000 wildebeest victims per year, but the wildebeest population of a million is producing several times that number of young each year, and they are quite long-lived animals. It is small wonder that at present their population is expanding quite fast, and that predation by lions does not prevent it, although it may slow it a little. This expansion cannot go on indefinitely, of course. When there is a very parched dry season, and so almost no adequate food, many wildebeest will die of starvation and their numbers will come down again sharply. Predation by lions thus has very little influence on the size of the wildebeest population, which is largely determined by the average rainfall and hence the distribution of their food. Perhaps five times as many wildebeest die of disease, old age, starvation, or any of these combined, as die through predation by lions.

Other predators are also preying on wildebeest, of course, hyaenas being the only species which takes more than a few, so predation has more impact than if only lions were involved. On the other hand, lions do not, in fact, feed solely on the wildebeest but on a whole range of other prey species too, all of which thus share the burden of predators' hunger.

Why are so (relatively) few wildebeest killed by lions? The answer probably lies in their feet! The huge herds are so mobile that few predators can follow them wherever they migrate, and indeed most predators remain permanently within their own territories. Thus for most of the year any particular pride's territory does not contain any wildebeest at all, and then for a very few months only it is deluged with them. Although at these feast times I have seen prides completely glutted, lying bloated beside uneaten kills, they can still make almost no impact on the hordes of gnus.

I have concentrated on the wildebeest because it is the commonest prey species around. As I mentioned in Chapter 6, on the whole lions take more zebras than wildebeest in the Serengeti; zebras are only about a third as common, but they are less unevenly distributed over the whole area and so some zebras are usually to be found in a greater number of lion territories. Predation presumably has more influence on them than it does on the wildebeest population, but nonetheless food availability is much more important.

In the same way the various prey species, such as the hartebeest, topi, impala and warthog, which are resident throughout the year in some lions' territory, probably bear a proportionately greater share of lions' attentions than do the migratory species. But these resident species share the load among them, and on the whole are alert and I think difficult to catch. They also gain some respite for perhaps half the year when zebras or wildebeest are in their area, for at that time the lions are much more likely to catch one of the latter two species. In a sense the migratory herds tend to buffer the residents against predation. I do not think that predation plays a significant part in controlling how many of these resident prey there may be in an area, with the possible exception of warthogs, which are killed at a surprisingly high rate considering their numbers. They are vulnerable because they seem to be careless and not as alert as most other ungulates, nor can they run as fast. On the other hand, they produce several young in a litter while the other prey species produce only one, so the high rate of predation on their piglets can be sustained.

If lions are killing only such a small proportion of the potential prey in the Serengeti, why are there not more lions there? First, there are the problems that not all prey are available within a pride's territory. Second, not all those that are present are catchable: it may be only a proportion of the prey which are sufficiently unalert or slow to be vulnerable to predation by lions. Third, lions seem to control their own numbers. When their pride gets larger, they tend to expel more sub-adult females, thus setting a top limit to the size of their pride. Why lions should have evolved a tendency to do this over the generations I do not really know. I guess that the point at which they decide (unconsciously) that a pride should not get any bigger has become tuned to the probable amount of food their territory might provide in a really bad season, which might occur only perhaps every ten, twenty or more years. It makes sense to expel surplus pride members when food is still abundant rather than a few years later when it is scarce; later the surplus lionesses will probably be more reluctant to go, older and more difficult to expel, and their slim chances of finding a suitable vacant area in which to found a new pride will be slimmer still.

Even if lions and other predators did take a much higher proportion of the prey populations, they might still have rather little effect on those prey, depending on which prey individuals they killed. Some lions' victims are very old or diseased; they would probably die fairly soon anyway, and lions only hasten the process, sometimes, I felt, mercifully. Also, as any farmer knows, many male animals are, in a sense, unnecessary, because a single bull, for example, can fertilize a large number of cows. Thousands of male wildebeest fall prey to lions each year, but their loss has no effect at all on the number of wildebeest calves born the next year; indeed the absence of these extra wildebeest mouths competing for sparse food may even result in better survival of those calves.

For these various reasons, then, lions on the whole have rather little direct effect on the number of prey animals in a region. Even the combined effect of all the carnivores is not the most important factor determining herbivore numbers, except perhaps of some of the scarcer prey species. I speak mainly of the Serengeti lions, but the same is probably true of most other large undisturbed areas where predators, prey and habitat have had time to adjust to one another.

Although the predators of the Serengeti do not control the numbers of their prey, they have had a tremendous influence on the evolution of those prey species. I have already said that ungulates are swift and alert; their speed and vigilance have been bred into them by the attention of predators. More accurately, any which were slow or drowsy would have ended up as lion food, leaving their fitter companions to pass on any genes which made them better able to avoid being caught. We have predators to thank for the tense yet graceful appearance of the impala, the wariness of the topi and the nimbleness of the gazelle.

As well as removing constitutionally deficient animals, lions also kill others which are temporarily unfit through disease. By doing so, they help to prevent disease from spreading, and they give an extra advantage to any animal which can develop an immunity from even relatively harmless infections. I did not often come across visibly sick animals, but of course this could have been for two reasons – either because they rarely become ill, or else because if they did they were captured quite soon.

Lions may well eliminate unusual individual animals too. It is partly

98 Zebras are striped at both ends, vertically at the front and horizontally behind. The exact pattern of markings is different on every individual

because it behaves differently that a sick animal is conspicuous, and it is possible that other kinds of conspicuousness would also be disadvantageous. When watching a herd of zebras with their vivid, almost dazzling, black and white coat patterns flickering in the sunlight, I often wondered why on earth they should be coloured like that. Other people have wondered the same, of course, and have suggested that they are well camouflaged among trees, or have pointed out that zebras are not conspicuous at dusk or at night. Although these explanations are unsatisfactory on all sorts of grounds, I cannot produce better ones as to why zebras' coats first became striped. But now that they *are* striped, we can make a good guess as to why they remain so. Any zebra which was born with a strikingly different coat colour would be more likely to be chosen and picked off by lions; it would be chosen either because conspicuousness so often indicates some kind of defect, or because a lion would be able to distinguish and aim at the animal more easily among a galloping horde of its striped companions fleeing after being ambushed. Even if the new coat colour provided slightly better camouflage than a striped one, it would put its wearer at much greater risk, and so the genes which cause this new colour would not get passed on to the next generation of zebras. Lions might thus effect a stabilizing

218

form of selection on their prey species in favour of average animals.

Apart from being wary, speedy, healthy and ordinary, what other behaviour would help a herbivore to avoid providing a lion's meal? One way is not to linger at danger spots such as watering places where ambushes by lions are possible. Drinking is probably the last action many antelopes perform. It was very noticeable that many species of herbivores were more timid when they were near a river. As I drove past, perhaps fifty yards from where they were drinking, they would often bolt away from the river, stream past the front of my landrover and then watch my progress from a similar distance away on the 'safe' side. Herbivores tend to choose clear open pools or river banks to drink from, if they can, but often in the dry season they have little choice.

A reasonably sure way of telling that a place is safe is if someone else has gone there and survived. Antelopes going down to water go hesitantly and tensely, and tend to wait some way away until a first one has started drinking; once it has, the rest follow quite quickly. Their behaviour often reminded me of a childhood story about penguins, none of whom wanted to be the first to dive off an ice floe into the sea where a hungry seal might be lurking to take the first animal. The same safety principle applies when animals are travelling, moving in lines one after the other. It is a fairly good bet that if one animal has just taken that path, a second one is unlikely to encounter a lion hidden upon it. In just the same way, the safest path through a minefield is to follow someone else's footprints. Animals are not necessarily conscious of why this should be, but natural selection would generally favour an antelope who tends to follow others rather than take a new route.

Wildebeest provide a particularly striking example of this kind of behaviour. In their long migrations they travel in long winding strings, loping, mile after mile, gnu after gnu, each following just where the one in front went. When the large herds had migrated through my area I would find it traversed by narrow bare trails, only about a foot wide, where tens of thousands of hooves had landed one after the other. When my course in my car happened to cross one of the lines of running wildebeest, the latter were apparently put into a dilemma; they wanted both to follow their leaders and also to avoid me, and consequently the landrover 'pushed' the line sideways rather like elastic. As I drove further on, the enforced bend in the running line got more and more pronounced, with wildebeest galloping desperately hard to get round past the front of my moving car. At last the line would snap, as some brave wildebeest decided to cut the corner and join his companions by crossing behind the car; he would be followed by others, and so the line would be re-formed again.

This almost blind following behaviour has evolved as a way of avoiding being preyed upon by lions – originality in an individual is selected against – but such following also has its costs to the species. When a travelling wildebeest herd comes to a river which has to be crossed on their migration, they gather into a large milling mooing mass, watching the crossing point until one takes the plunge, literally, swims across, and rushes out on the other side. The next follows at once, and the next, and the next few thousands. All try to get across the river and out as quickly as possible, to reduce the time when they are at risk of falling easy prey to lions. The lions know that wildebeest crossing rivers are virtually a free meal, and they often move quickly to a point where they see a herd crossing. The wildebeest follow one another so quickly that if one stumbles it is quite likely to get landed on by the next, pushed under, trampled and perhaps drowned by the later crossers; because they each have to hurry for fear of lions, they each have to hurry even more for fear of being trampled underhoof by the next. Thus lion predation has started a vicious circle, which results in a large number of wildebeest perishing accidentally through the haste of their companions. A number of times I came across places where several or even dozens of wildebeest had drowned in this way during their crossing of a harmless river.

Small calves are particularly at risk, being weaker than adults. Alan Root told me how lions indirectly caused the deaths of well over a thousand wildebeest calves at Lake Lagarja by ambushing a herd which was crossing a stream at a good crossing point near its inflow into the lake. The wildebeest therefore started to swim across the lake at a wide point further along. They are quite good swimmers, even the calves, but problems arose because the calves could not swim quite as fast as their mothers. A cow would arrive at the further shore and find her calf was not with her. Sometimes she waited, sometimes she followed the rest of the wildebeest away from the lake, and sometimes she swam back again to look for it, but I think perhaps wildebeest find it difficult to recognize one another's heads while swimming. The calf would then arrive at the further side of the lake, and might do any of the three things its mother did. As a result, thousands of wildebeest calves got separated from their mothers, some only temporarily, but many of them permanently and therefore fatally; they died from exhaustion in the water or of starvation on the land.

The vulnerability of their calves is probably one of the reasons why the Serengeti wildebeest give birth when they are out on the open plains where there are few rivers to be crossed. There are other reasons too, of course: the plains provide less cover for the ambushing predators, and consist of more nutritive grasses. In addition, that is where all the other wildebeest and their calves are too, providing a measure of protection by their sheer abundance. They all give birth at about the same time, probably because any calves born early or late are more conspicuous and more likely to be hunted by hyaenas than those born in the middle of the birth season when there are thousands of other potential victims all around. The young of any animal are, of course, at risk soon after birth, but the calves of many of the antelopes are able to run at speed within an astonishingly short time of their birth, because those which did not in the past were much more likely to be caught by predators.

There is safety in numbers for three rather different reasons. First, many eyes, ears and nostrils are better than a single pair at detecting an approaching lion or other enemy. It was probably for this reason that I often came across small mixed groups of territorial male antelopes – a male topi, hartebeest and impala, perhaps. Each animal would keep others of the same species out of its own territory, yet often stayed close to a territorial male of a different species. Similarly, I quite often saw a baboon troop feeding intermingled with a herd of impalas, and it has been suggested that by staying together they both benefit – the baboons have good eyesight and colour vision, while the impalas probably have a better sense of smell. Most antelopes, unless they are territorial males, are usually with companions of the same species, and hence I saw groups or herds of them together. George Schaller found that lions' hunts were more likely to be successful if the target was a lone animal than if it was a group, probably because the latter contained more alert individuals to detect the hunters.

A second reason for a prey animal to be in a group is if by doing so it can join forces with others to keep predators away. It is possible that this happens with groups of buffaloes facing lions, and it also happens with baboons facing leopards. A group of male baboons would make short work of a leopard which tried openly to seize one of their number, and I have seen them threatening leopards when they encountered them. If the wildebeest were all to unite, they could probably wipe all the lions and other predators off the Serengeti; it would involve a number of them dying in the process, but fewer, I would guess, than are killed by lions every year, and then they would have a lifetime of peace.

However, such behaviour cannot evolve, because any wildebeest which started attacking lions would very quickly be killed by one. Natural selection cannot favour behaviour which harms the individual animal performing it, even if it were for the good of the species as a whole (unless it helped that individual's relatives a disproportionate amount). Neither zebras nor wildebeest defend their young against lions, and the risk involved would be enormous. They do defend them against the much smaller hyaenas, however, and both stallion and mare zebras will take part in this, where the risk to their own life is much less. Zebras live in stable family groups, so a foal is accompanied by both its parents. By contrast, no wildebeest bull knows who his offspring are, even if he ever met them among the multitude, and so no male wildebeest defends calves.

There is a third and more selfish reason why it is a good thing for an antelope to be part of a group, even if that group is no better at detecting or fending off lions or other predators. Suppose that a lioness stalks towards one or a group of impalas, with a 20 per cent chance of being successful in her hunt. An impala on his own has a one-fifth chance of perishing. An impala with nine companions is much safer – it is most likely that it will be one of his companions who ends up inside a lion, so his chance of dying is now only one-fiftieth. Thus it would be well worthwhile for an impala to be with a group, even if groups provided lions with easier meals rather than more difficult ones. The same principle of buffering oneself with companions who may get eaten instead is probably a widespread cause contributing towards grouping by prey animals.

COMPETITORS

I have referred in passing to some of the lions' competitors in the Serengeti – animals which also eat the meat of the prey species on which lions feed. Here I want to consider lions' interactions with these competing species a little more closely, starting with the most closely related of these, the leopard, which I have described in Chapter 7. Lions chase a leopard if they come across one, but the latter usually escapes into a tree; several times I came across an *Acacia* with a leopard in the top and a lion at the bottom. On their part, a leopard will kill a small lion cub if it finds one unguarded: I have seen a leopard feeding on the carcass of a lion cub, and I think they kill them mainly for food as

99 A leopard rests in cool dappled shade, camouflaged and easily overlooked in a leafy tree

they do many other small animals. By contrast a lion chasing a leopard has the hostile facial expression it has when threatening one of its own species, rather than its alert attentive face as when hunting prey, and lions apparently do not eat a leopard if they manage to catch it. Thus lions treat leopards as enemies, while leopards treat lions either as attackers to be avoided or as a meal to be consumed.

The larger lions may rob leopards of their kills, but on the whole the leopard's technique of carrying them up into trees, storing and eating them there ensures that they lose few of them through plunder by lions. Leopards will also scavenge meat from carcasses which they have not killed themselves, in the same way as lions do, but to a lesser extent; they do not get an appreciable amount from lion kills. The two species are not in serious ecological competition with one another, for the leopard's prey species and those of the lion do not overlap much, partly because they tend to hunt in somewhat different habitats, by different methods and at different times of day. Both take warthogs, impalas and gazelles quite frequently, leopards killing more young of these species, while lions largely take adults. These form only a small part of a lion's

223

diet but a greater proportion of that of a leopard. I think lions influence leopards more than vice versa. If all leopards were to be removed, this would make virtually no difference to the lion population. On the other hand the disappearance of lions would probably make life fractionally easier for leopards; they would be robbed less often, and would run less risk of being attacked suddenly by a hostile larger predator, but they would probably find it little easier to catch their food supply. They might use the area differently and come out into the open more, further away from the thicker vegetation which at present offers them protection and a food supply.

In Chapter 8 I described the way of life of the cheetah and how it interacts with lions, from whom it keeps far away whenever it can. The relationship is even more one-sided than was the case with leopards. Lions chase cheetahs and kill their cubs if they find them; they also rob cheetahs of their kills quite often, the cheetah being unable either to defend its meal or to get it out of reach of lions. On the other hand, no cheetah ever threatens or even approaches lions voluntarily, nor does it scavenge meat from animals which it has not killed itself; thus a cheetah does not deprive lions of any food, but provides them with a small amount. This amount is extremely small from the lion's point of view, but more significant from the cheetah's, and is an extra burden adding to an already difficult way of life for the high-speed cat. The two species are not in serious ecological competition with one another because cheetahs are very scarce while their main food supply, the gazelles, are abundant, and are little fed on by lions. In addition, cheetahs do not restrict their movements to small defined territories as lions and leopards do, but follow their migrating food concentrations over the plains and out of the territories of resident larger cats. However, this does not take them beyond the range of hyaenas, which probably offer more competition than lions. Hyaenas are more abundant than lions, more alert in detecting and running towards vultures gathering near a cheetah kill, and include in their diet a higher proportion of gazelles which are the cheetah's principal food.

Spotted hyaenas have cropped up at intervals throughout this book. They are the most abundant of the large carnivores in the Serengeti as a whole, there being about 4000 of them or roughly twice as many as there are lions in the region. They are more creatures of open country than of woodland, however, and I estimate that in my study area there were only a third as many as lions. Hyaenas are formidable animals, weighing just over a hundredweight, powerful and solid. Their hind-

100 An elderly spotted hyaena, a carnivore which hunts in packs at night and kills large prey animals. Hyaenas also scavenge much food very efficiently from carcasses of animals which have died of other causes

quarters are lower than their shoulders, giving them a somewhat skulking appearance which, I think, is one of the reasons for their having been variously maligned, despised or disliked in the past. Their appearance, and their propensity to scavenge, has caused them to be labelled as cowardly – 'hyaena' is still used as a term of abuse. The cause of the relatively small hindquarters is really the relatively large shoulders and powerful thick neck; I have seen hyaenas carrying and running fast with quite heavy pieces of carcass. They are very strong runners: they can keep up a steady loping gait for miles, and they can also maintain a high speed run of thirty to thirty-five mph for long distances. The hyaena family, or *Hyaenidae*, are intermediate between the dog and cat families and actually more closely related to the latter, but in their running abilities they are much more similar to the dogs.

Hyaenas certainly scavenge, but they are certainly not only scavengers, and in some places not mainly scavengers. Hans Kruuk, who studied them in Ngorongoro and the Serengeti, found that they are efficient hunters, able to capture and kill adult prey animals as large as

225

wildebeest and zebras. They do most of their hunting at night, and most of it in packs, and they catch their prey by running it down after a long chase. These packs are temporary groups of hyaenas which have gathered for a hunt, others often joining in once a chase has started, and more join to feed on the resulting carcass. Smaller packs tend to hunt smaller, more vulnerable prey. Hyaenas will hunt alone too, but Kruuk showed that they were less effective at doing so – for example, a mother wildebeest could defend her young against a single pursuer but not against two.

The social organization of hyaenas is also flexible. In Ngorongoro, where they are abundant, they live in what Kruuk called clans, containing between thirty and eighty adults and occupying and defending a large group territory. They mark the boundary of this territory by depositing their droppings at a number of 'latrine' points along it, and by pasting vegetation with a secretion from their anal glands. Hyaenas drive out intruders if they encounter them, and large-scale territorial clashes between neighbouring clans may take place. One night I was attracted by the loud whooping and giggling noises of many hyaenas to the carcass of a wildebeest bull, which two rival clans were contesting. There were at least twenty on each side. While one group was feeding, the others gathered some fifty yards away; after several minutes they ran forward as a line, their short black tails stuck up in the air and their aggressively raised heads making them lope in a surprisingly rocking manner. The feeders were chased off or fled, and the assailants ate hurriedly until the ousted clan in turn regrouped and turned the tables in the same way. As a result the carcass changed possession five times in forty minutes. Some of the skirmishing took place some distance from the carcass, and I got the impression that it was as much a territorial boundary which was being disputed as a meal.

On the whole most of the Serengeti hyaenas are less tied to their territories than the Ngorongoro ones. Many follow the migratory herds of zebras and wildebeest over long distances. Others have dens containing cubs at the edges of the plains, so they commute many miles from there to the prey concentrations and back again to feed their young with milk. They do not regurgitate meat for them, nor carry back pieces of food; as a result young hyaenas are reared on milk alone for much longer than lion cubs. The dens are usually old warthog holes, expanded by further digging by hyaenas, particularly the cubs. They are used communally, by more than one female and cubs, but hyaenas do not suckle one another's young as lions do and they produce only

101 Two spotted hyaenas. Note their powerful shoulders and necks. A pack of hyaenas is more than a match for a single lion

two in a litter. The two sexes look almost identical, which gave rise to the age-old but erroneous belief that hyaenas are hermaphrodites and, it was even suggested, this is what makes them laugh so much.

It is the loud laughter when squabbling at carcasses which attracts other hyaenas and other scavengers to the spot, as it did me in the incident I have described. A feeding gathering with many hyaenas present can produce a cacophony of whoops, yells and giggles. This is audible from a long distance away, and often lures lions to the spot. A group of them can usually take over a carcass from a pack of hyaenas, and indeed Kruuk found that this was the main way in which lions in Ngorongoro were obtaining their food. In my area, with many fewer hyaenas and more lions, the latter got virtually none of their food from hyaenas.

It is not an easy task for lions to deprive hyaenas of a carcass. Males, being larger and bolder, are able to do it more than lionesses, and both sexes are more likely both to try and to succeed if they are with companions rather than on their own. Nevertheless, a pack of hyaenas can sometimes drive even a group of lions from a carcass; they rarely do so if it was the lions who made the kill, mainly because there are unlikely to be many hyaenas gathered nearby, but they may dispossess lions who have temporarily taken over their carcass. Hyaenas sometimes mob or chase lions at other times too, for no apparent cause. I have found a lioness taking refuge in a tree from a noisy group of a dozen hyaenas below; and one elderly lioness died of wounds all over her hindquarters which only hyaenas could have inflicted. The latter sometimes kill and eat lion cubs, while on the other hand, lions sometimes catch and kill hyaenas but do not eat them. Nothing likes hyaena meat much, not even vultures; I do not know why.

Lions provide hyaenas with some food. Although a lion pride usually leaves little meat on its kills, sometimes there is an appreciable quantity which hyaenas find before vultures do. Hyaenas can also make use of what is left even after lions and vultures have removed almost all traces of meat. They readily eat the skin of even the larger prey animals, cutting their way along the edges of it rather like a caterpillar along the edge of a leaf and consuming large quantities of hair which they later regurgitate. Hyaenas also have remarkable bone-crushing teeth; these they use to break and eat bones which lions have left, to consume the bone marrow inside. Their digestive system is remarkable, enabling them to dissolve the pieces of bone they have eaten, extracting the protein matrix around which bones are made for their own use and excreting the inorganic part as hard white chalk-like lumps. No other carnivore in the Serengeti can do this; although lions swallow bone fragments, these reappear unaltered and unutilized in their droppings.

102 Two of a pack of wild dogs, small but highly efficient carnivores which hunt by day by running down their prey. They live in permanent close-knit packs and show a high degree of co-operation with one another

These abilities are part of the reason why hyaenas are more efficient scavengers than lions, and therefore why they scavenge more. They are more efficient, too, in their locomotion, being able to travel over much longer distances, both faster and with less effort; thus they can find carcasses sooner than lions and so get more from them. Each species deprives the other of some scavenging opportunities.

As predators, on the other hand, lions and hyaenas compete in a different way. To some extent they take different species, partly because hyaenas are found particularly on the plains and lions more in the woodlands. Hyaenas feed most on wildebeest, somewhat on gazelles, a little on zebra and very little on all the other species combined. On the other hand lions in the Serengeti as a whole feed most on zebras, closely followed by wildebeest, scarcely on gazelles, but appreciably on a whole range of other species including warthog, buffalo, kongoni, impala, giraffe, eland and topi. Where the two predators' diets overlap, in both including a sizeable proportion of wildebeest, the segment of the prey population they catch differs in line with their differing hunting methods. Thus hyaenas, which capture their victims by running them down, get a high proportion of calves and sick animals because these run less fast or tire sooner. Lions, hunting by ambushing unsuspecting prey, get few calves but many completely healthy adults. I doubt whether the ecological competition between them is great.

Wild dogs compete with lions even less. These intriguing animals are scarce, there being probably fewer than two hundred of them in the whole Serengeti area. They are more social than hyaenas or even lions, living in small cohesive packs of up to about a dozen adults and as many more young. Their coat, predominantly black and white and brown markings, provides an excellent means of recognizing different individuals and so of keeping long-term records of the fortunes of a number of packs, which have been observed for over twelve years by Hugo van Lawick, James Malcolm, and George and Lory Frame. A pack has a dominant pair of dogs, with usually only this one female producing young – between ten and sixteen pups in a litter. The whole pack helps to rear the puppies, guarding them and regurgitating meat for them.

The members of wild dog packs do not drift off separately and rejoin one another in the loose way that both lions and hyaenas do; they stay together all the time except when some dogs stay with puppies while others hunt. Hunting is essentially a group activity for catching and killing their prey and subsequently for guarding it. Prey is caught in the typical dog fashion through a long-distance daytime chase which is a magnificent spectacle to watch as the smooth running dark dogs race over the ground, some ahead of others and some further to the side. What makes them select one particular prey animal to chase I do not know, but soon all the dogs are pursuing the same one, usually a gazelle. When, after perhaps a mile of running at about thirty-five mph, the gazelle begins to tire it may start to circle or zig-zag, which is not a useful defence against a group of pursuers since the later dogs can cut the corners. One seizes it and it is quickly killed and consumed, the young taking precedence over the adults which stand nearby keeping hyaenas away.

The commonest prey of wild dogs are gazelles, these being both abundant and in the size range that the dogs can easily deal with; an adult dog weighs only about 40 lb. They also kill wildebeest calves in the appropriate season, and occasional large prey such as adult zebra or wildebeest if no other smaller victims are obtainable. The comparatively rare killing of such large victims by such small predators is a slow and painful process to observe, and is part of the reason why wild dogs have been so often vilified and persecuted by people who should know better. This persecution has contributed to the scarcity of the wild dog, but it is not the only cause. It is curious that the two species with the highest success rates in their hunting – the cheetah and wild dog – should also be the two least common species of the larger predators; perhaps the very demanding hunting method of both species is responsible. Both are too scarce to offer one another any appreciable competition, despite feeding on the same prey species. Indeed in the very long term they may even help one another by making it impossible for gazelles to evolve a defence against either; it is difficult for a gazelle to be both enough of a sprinter to outpace a cheetah and enough of a long-distance runner to outrun wild dogs.

Lions rarely come into contact with wild dogs who, like hyaenas, tend to stay more on the plains, travelling long distances either erratically or to and from their den if they have small pups. Their prey scarcely overlaps at all with that of lions, nor do they scavenge significantly.

Vultures do, and are entirely dependent on it. There are six species of vulture in the Serengeti, but the two griffon vultures are by far the commonest. These large birds are superbly equipped to be efficient scavengers. All day they travel almost effortlessly over an enormous area, ascending in circles in thermal upcurrents and gliding along and slightly downwards between one and the next; for hours on end they

103 A vulture plummets down towards a carcass it has detected. Other vultures, lions and hyaenas also watch vultures descending, and so are often led to the carcass too

have no need to beat their wings. With sharp eyesight they scan the ground below for a carcass, and watch the behaviour of other soaring vultures which may have spotted one. A dead animal once found is soon almost submerged beneath a mass of vultures, some feeding and others trying to. No land scavenger can hope to travel over and scan an area as efficiently. It can, however, make use of the vultures as a pointer to a food source, as both lions and hyaenas do. Many times I have seen the earth-bound animal arrive too late to gain any food, but often it gains at least a small meal for its pains. On the whole, vultures deprive lions of

104 As soon as lions leave a carcass all the waiting griffon vultures converge on it in a seething hissing mass

105 A lioness runs in and drives vultures from a carcass

more food than they lead them to, and a purely scavenging way of life would be more possible for a carnivorous mammal if these birds had not already taken it.

Lions provide vultures with only a small amount of food; carcasses of animals which have died of natural causes are far more important to the birds. Predators guard their kills until most of the meat is consumed; when they leave, vultures can sometimes get a little more from the carcass, but the griffon vultures cannot use skin or bone as hyaenas do.

Vultures provide many mental torments for lions. Several times I have seen this when a lion has a kill in the open too heavy to drag to the shade. The lion has had a meal but wants to feed again later when he is less full and the day less hot. He is uncomfortable in the sun and retreats towards the shade a little way away. As he goes the waiting vultures run and fly in to the carcass. He sees this and rushes back to chase them off, and they disperse to about thirty yards away and wait until he starts to leave again. Back and forth he goes like a yo-yo, and eventually he gives up the uneven struggle. Lions seem unable to bear seeing vultures feeding even from carcasses they have finished with. Several times I saw lions leave the remains of a kill and walk a considerable distance away, only to run back again when they saw vultures gathering at it.

One other way in which lions supply a little vulture food is through their droppings. Often I would see a few of the small hooded vultures in the trees near a resting pride of lions which had no kill. Some people have suggested that they are waiting for the lions to acquire one, but this is clearly not the case: in fact they are waiting to eat any lion droppings. Vultures' digestive systems are more efficient than lions'; the big cats' droppings contain pieces of tough skin or other tissue, semi-digested meat and gut parasites, all of which help to provide a meal for these remarkable birds.

Other animals also get a little food from lion kills. Jackals treat lions as they do leopards and cheetahs by yapping shrilly at them. They get most of their food by their own foraging and hunting efforts but, like vultures, they get the occasional meal from lion-killed and lion-left carcasses. The jackal has been called 'the lion's provider', but for no valid reason that I could see in the Serengeti, for lions get no food through the help or the small kills of jackals.

There are a variety of other birds, apart from vultures, which take pieces of meat from carcasses, and so are supplied to a small extent by lions. Among them are marabou storks, tawny eagles, whitenaped

106 A zebra carcass when vultures and jackals have finished with it. The bones are picked clean, the skin removed and the forelimbs separated. Hyaenas if hungry will crack the bones and extract more food from them

107 a&b A well-fed lion cub leaves a little-eaten wildebeest carcass, and at once jackals come in to take a share, wary and alert for the possible return of a lion

ravens, and occasionally starlings. All feed mainly on other foods, for they could not compete with the vultures. The smaller birds, however, have the advantage of being able to take off much more quickly than the gliding-adapted vultures, and several times I have seen them able to feed on a carcass when the lions were still too close for the vultures to risk trying to do so.

NUISANCES

As we have seen, lions have no real enemies or significant rivals among other species in their environment. This does not mean that life is necessarily all easy for them, for they have both enemies and rivals within their own species, and they have to come into contact with prey animals larger than themselves. They also have to cope with a variety of far smaller animals which are a considerable nuisance to their well-being.

Flies are a major nuisance. A lion at rest, especially if he is near a carcass, sometimes has flies swarming all over him. His closed eyelids prevent the insects from doing more than sucking the moisture around the edges of his eyes. The hairy insides to his ears make it difficult for flies to crawl into them, but even so he has to flick his ears often as an irritating fly starts to get through the barrier. This was sometimes useful to me, because the flicking of a dark ear could be the first indication that lions were nearby. At intervals the lion shakes its head, rather as a dog will, with a flapping of its ears, and a swarm of flies separates from its body and settles back onto it again. I think it is partly to avoid flies that lions are more active when it is cooler, and that they sometimes go up into trees to rest.

There are a number of different kinds of flies, and they affect lions in a variety of ways. The ordinary housefly type does not bite or hurt, merely crawls and irritates. Its larvae feed on meat and breed in carcasses which are not eaten by other scavengers; without vultures the air would probably be even thicker with flies. The small 'wildebeest fly' breeds in wildebeest droppings; although a lion's coat may in patches be darkened by a crowd of these little flies, he seems largely oblivious to them. Other flies bite, however. One type, *Stomoxys*, suck a lion's blood from weak parts of its anatomy. These are partly responsible for the progressive enlargement of nicks in lions' ears, for their attentions can keep small wounds open, and the edges of the ears, especially in old animals, are often somewhat devoid of hair and thus vulnerable to attack.

Tsetse flies also cause trouble for lions. These are quite large flies, with painful sharp bites as I have experienced innumerable times; sometimes, however, they managed to engorge themselves without my noticing, and then they would fly off like pregnant helicopters to rest and convert my valuable blood into new insects. They feed on lions in the same way. The lion strongly resents their presence, flicks its skin and its tail, and often attempts to bite at the offending insects, which is rather like trying to catch swallows with a butterfly net. Some tsetse flies carry and transmit the agents responsible for sleeping sickness: trypanosomes are minute parasites which live in the blood of infected mammals, and can be lethal to those susceptible to the disease, including humans and some of their cattle. It is sleeping sickness which has been mainly responsible in the past for keeping the Serengeti empty of human inhabitants. Most species of wild animal are scarcely affected by the disease, although a few carry the parasites in their blood. I was asked to immobilize a large number of lions and hyaenas to determine whether these animals might be a potential reservoir of the human disease. It turned out that almost all adult lions in the Serengeti are infected by trypanosomes, apparently without ill effect, although the parasites presumably contribute an extra burden which may be negligible except in times of stress or starvation. It is curious that lions (and hyaenas) are more likely to be infected than other animals, for tsetse flies do not bite them much more often. It seems likely that the predators become infected through eating infected prey; thus lions may act not so much as a reservoir of the disease themselves as a drain which eliminates many other potential reservoirs.

Trypanosomes are not the only parasite with which lions are infected. There are a number of other bacteria and protozoa which are found in perfectly healthy adult lions, but which would probably horrify most vets. Lions also contain various worms in their intestines, and indeed fresh lion droppings sometimes contain tapeworm segments – thus the little hooded vultures may even be slightly beneficial to lions by eating their droppings, and so perhaps reducing fractionally the chances of other lions becoming infected.

Ticks are an external parasite – small crab-like animals related to spiders, which attach themselves to a mammal's skin and slowly suck its blood. Most lions I examined when immobilized had one or two of these ticks somewhere on the body, but in nowhere near the numbers I

236

108 Flies are a frequent nuisance to a lion in the daytime. The only defence is to seek cool shade, blow them out of the nostrils, shut them out of the eyes and flick them out of the ears

would see attached to the soft skin regions of animals such as buffaloes and giraffes, despite the attentions of the little oxpecker birds who presumably removed some. Lions' frequent grooming, of themselves and of one another, seem to keep them largely free of external parasites.

There is one exception, however. Almost every lion I saw had several or many fat little yellow flies called hippoboscids running about among its hair, particularly in the sheltered parts around the groin and in the foreleg pits. As the lion rolled over on its back, exposing a different part of its belly, the little hippoboscid flies exposed there would scurry over the body or delve into the hair and conceal themselves again. They can fly, but rarely do. They presumably feed on the lion's blood, yet I never saw a lion pay any attention to them at all. The only animal which did was a small lizard living on a kopje which one pride of lions often frequented; I saw it repeatedly jumping up onto the prostrate body of a sleeping lion and catching these round and succulent looking flies, the lion being apparently oblivious of its presence.

Humans and lions are both effective predators on other animals, although by different techniques, so to some extent they compete with one another, directly and indirectly, rather as hyaenas and lions do. The most direct kind of competition is seen in man-eating by lions. I must stress that this is abnormal behaviour by lions, but nonetheless it captures people's attention. There have been a number of famous man-eating lions, the best known being two who terrorized (and consumed many of) the labour force involved with building a railway through Tsavo in Kenya at the end of last century, until Colonel Patterson eventually managed to shoot them. Most man-eating lions are finally killed by man, and this must maintain a strong selection against lions who take to feeding on this defenceless prey. Such behaviour is rare, and usually its origin is unknown. It seems that once a lion has for some reason killed and fed on humans, and so knows that they are harmless, easy prey and good edible meat, he is liable to continue to do so. A lion at Lake Manyara National Park started haunting the rubbish dump by a local village; there he would have come into contact extensively with human smells, and lost his fear of them. One night, apparently, a drunken villager lurching and behaving quite abnormally was seized by this lion onto which he may even have stumbled, and was killed and then eaten. The lion subsequently ate two more people in the next few months before he could be identified and destroyed.

In some ways it is surprising that humans are not killed by lions much more commonly, for we are a weak and slow species. But our culture enables us to do what the wildebeest cannot: humans can co-operate and, although at some personal risk, can benefit their species by destroying a lion which is preying on it. Such dangerous unselfish behaviour for the good of the community cannot evolve in prey species which do not have a high degree of co-ordination within compact social groups.

The shoe is often on the other foot, however, and humans kill a great many more lions than vice versa. They do so for a variety of motives. The young Masai warriors demonstrate their manhood by hunting lions, surrounding one and killing it armed only with spears. It is undoubtedly a test of courage, and the highest honour goes to him who first seizes the lion's tail; but it is said that even more blood is spilled in subsequent disputes over who grabbed the tail first than through the

109 A young male lion, shot for sport and now stuffed and mounted, stares with glass eyes through zebra skin handbags in a curio shop

teeth and claws of the lion itself. Lion hunts of this sort are now prohibited, and so rarely take place. The more modern equivalent is for a wealthy man to shoot lions for 'sport' which requires much less skill or courage, particularly as the licensed 'white hunter' in charge of his shooting safari is on hand to cover up for any mistakes he may make. Such sportsmen nowadays shoot only one or two lions, but in the last hundred years many people shot dozens of them.

Other people kill lions for other reasons. There are obscure tribes of people who frequently eat lion meat, for example. This, incidentally, can be delicious, as I tasted when I kept for consumption the haunch of a healthy young lioness killed by an adult lion during a territorial clash. The surprisingly white meat was inadvertently eaten with relish too by a friend who adamantly refused to eat lion but also refused to believe me when I told him which was lion and which pork! Various pieces of a lion's anatomy are supposed to have medicinal or magical value: I was twice asked to provide the small and degenerate clavicle or collar bone of a lion, for some purpose which I could not understand but which caused the asker some embarrassment.

Lions quite often get killed accidentally in poachers' snares which have been set for other animals, partly because they are attracted to the place by the corpses of these other animals. Therefore in an area where poaching is rife the lion population soon disappears, even before their food supply has likewise gone.

In agricultural areas lions are soon eliminated, for two reasons. The first is that they tend to prey on cattle, which are the most vulnerable victims imaginable with their senses apparently as slow as their legs. One morning in my study area I radio-tracked a pride of lions and found them feeding on three dark brown carcasses which took me some time to identify as cows, so unexpected were they. A cattle-stealing party of Masai youths had been crossing through the park at night with their spoils which the lions managed to surprise and make short work of. The Masai and other pastoral tribes usually protect their cattle at night by driving them into a 'boma' or ring of high thorn hedge which a lion cannot penetrate.

The second reason for the elimination of lions by farming is that the available lion food is removed by such activity. Herbivores which would feed on a farmer's crops are either destroyed or kept out by fencing. The small prey animals which remain can provide food for occasional leopards but not for prides of lions. As a result the range of the lion has shrunk enormously over the past two thousand years. Their disappearance from most of Europe before this time was mainly due to the spreading of forest over much of the countryside. By the time of Christ the last lions had just about died out from Greece, but others were still distributed through much of the Middle East to India. The Gir Forest in India now contains the fewer than two hundred last remaining Asiatic lions; throughout the rest of Asia they no longer exist. This century too has seen the extermination of the lion at the two ends of Africa; neither the Cape Lion nor the Barbary Lion subspecies exists any longer, although traces of their genes may perhaps be detected in the belly manes of lions which have been bred in captivity in European zoos for centuries.

Lions are still quite widely distributed in savannah country south of the Sahara desert. Their range is steadily being reduced, however, as a growing human population takes over such areas for settlement. In time the only regions which retain lion populations will be the national parks or game reserves which contain sufficient stocks of large herbivores. Although in the short term there are many such areas with abundant lions, in the long term lions may find their range in the wild reduced far below that of the differently endangered leopard. I suspect that my grandchildren will not hear of lions except in certain areas designated and protected as national parks.

Why lions should be conserved even there is a question which can be answered in many different ways. We have no moral right to treat this

110 A tourist minibus follows (too close) a moving lioness. Tourists would generally see more happening if they stayed further away and watched with binoculars, for their attentions spoil many hunts and interfere with some kinds of behaviour

planet of ours as ours alone; we would be ludicrously shortsighted if we allowed something to disappear which we can never recreate; and if we were to let this happen we would be scorned as well as pitied and abused for it by future generations who will want to observe nature still more than many of us do. Enormous numbers of tourists visit national parks in Africa, and the flow will expand much further still. With these visitors comes much-needed revenue, so investing in wildlife areas by African countries may produce one of the most lucrative of returns on the capital spent. And what the tourists are most eager to see are the large cat predators – lions, leopards and cheetahs. I would make a wild estimate that two long-lived leopardesses at Seronera have together probably been photographed nearly a quarter of a million times. Certainly they and their environment have brought enormous pleasure to a huge and growing number of people, myself among them.

To conserve an area such as the Serengeti requires much more than the drawing of a line on a map. The park wardens have arduous as well as rewarding tasks in preventing poaching, regulating fires, building roads, controlling tourists, supervising scientists, and managing the infra-structure needed for all these tasks. They may also have to manage the wildlife. Among the many kinds of wildlife management decisions which have to be made are for example whether disease should be combated; whether injured animals should be treated, put down or ignored; whether particularly rare species should be specially assisted; and whether reductions in the numbers of any species of animal are necessary, and if so how they should best be carried out. Some of these decisions are extremely difficult and highly controversial. On the whole the general feeling in most East African national parks, and I think rightly, is that as little management as possible should be done, that nature should be allowed to take its course unless very drastic changes in habitat are being caused, as for example through widespread tree destruction by elephants. It is usually felt that 'cosmetic' management is out of place in a national park.

One decision park wardens have had to make in the Serengeti is what to do about starving lion cubs. During bad dry seasons in the Seronera region, for example, the cubs of the two resident lion prides there sometimes get very little food from the small and occasional kills made by the adult lions, and may starve to death. They take a long time to do so, and present a pathetic spectacle during that time. They are unafraid of vehicles, for they live in a tourist area, and so they are seen at close range by visitors, who frequently urge the park wardens to alleviate the cubs' misery by feeding them. This, obviously, is what compassion makes any of us want to do. Yet I do not think it should be done; this is not because I am a callous scientist who is oblivious to the suffering of miserable animals while in ruthless pursuit of my data, but because making us feel better ourselves is really the only justification for our feeding lion cubs, and this is not sufficient justification.

Consider the various possible courses of action. To purchase cattle from a meat-hungry human population outside the park to feed to lions inside it – who have on average some one thousand large prey animals on the hoof available to each lion – is politically unacceptable, and would understandably alienate the local people. To do the lionesses' job for them, by shooting zebras or wildebeest inside the park and transporting the carcasses to the starving cubs, is another possibility. But by what right do we start loosing off bullets at peaceful groups of zebras? How much is it going to make zebras lose their present wonderful unconcern about vehicles near them? Are lions' lives more 'valuable' than zebras', and if so, why? How do we justify preventing the poaching of meat for human consumption and then killing those same animals for lions to eat? Lions are not in danger of dying out, and indeed the starvation of some of their cubs is to some extent a reflection of the fact that the Serengeti is full of lions, and that cubs' starvation is one of the ways in which their numbers are prevented from soaring.

If the starving cubs were enabled to survive, they would probably be expelled from the pride when adult and perhaps starve elsewhere, just as painfully but unseen by human eyes and therefore not troubling human consciences. Do we mean just to offer them postponed starvation? And should we not make the offer, too, to the many more lion cubs starving undetected elsewhere in the Serengeti? The answer to that is certainly 'No', because it is impossible on that scale, in the same way that it is impossible to do anything for the thousands of lost and so doomed wildebeest calves each year. If supplying food to starving lion cubs makes no difference to lion numbers in the future, this implies that more lions are dying of other causes instead, so our action has achieved little except to cause the death of different individual lions. If, on the other hand, lion numbers increase because of our kindness, there will be more starving lion cubs posing an even greater problem in the future. No course of action or inaction is wholly satisfactory, and in my view the least unsatisfactory one is to do nothing – not to try to interfere in a perfectly natural situation which arises solely as a byproduct of the lions' system of organizing their society and regulating their numbers.

There are other difficult management problems concerning lions. For example, if it has been decided after due consideration not to feed starving lion cubs, should they be put out of their distress by killing them quickly and painlessly. The same question, of course, applies to wildebeest with broken legs, and to many other animals with other ailments which are also likely to prove fatal. Again, I think we must consider what to do in the context of millions of animals in an environment where thousands of them are suffering and dying every year, mostly unseen. One does not solve the problem by despatching the few sufferers one happens to know of, although I appreciate that this argument can always be a recipe for inaction. But the subject of euthanasia for wildlife in national parks is awkward. Most lion cubs at Seronera, for example, are likely to go through a lean period at some stage, when they and their companions are near starvation and quite likely to die, so to put them down to save them from suffering would ensure that the lion prides at Seronera did not manage to raise any young. The point is that some cubs do survive, despite all the odds – and some of these have the odds very highly stacked against them. At one point during my time in the Serengeti, the park warden and veterinarian went out mercifully (and against my advice) to shoot two starving lion cubs whose chances of survival were rated at zero: the cubs were naked, weak, provoking protests from visitors about the authorities' indifference to suffering, and VIP visitors were expected. However, the warden could not find the cubs, who must have managed to crawl to cover. One of the cubs I never saw again, but the other survived somehow, and indeed was one of only two cubs to have been successfully raised by the Seronera pride during the early years of my study. She is now a mother, and I feel ought to be wearing a label telling of her fortunate escape from humane sentiments, and making visitors and park wardens realize, and think deeply about, the considerable problems surrounding human interference.

It is impossible to be sure that a lion is bound to die, for their tenacity to life is remarkable. I saw one old nomadic lioness who was almost unable to walk, whose teeth were worn down and whose ribs made her flanks deeply corrugated. She was obviously just on the point of death, so I was amazed when a full nine months later she turned up in a similar state thirty miles away. Where she had been or how she had survived in the meantime I do not know. She did not surprise me a second time, however, and after four days in the same place there she died.

In another exceptional instance I think our human interference *was* justified. A prime adult lioness, Masai female 14, lost all the skin along the middle two-thirds of her tail. How this happened I can only guess; I have a suspicion that her tail might have been run over by a tourist vehicle, but it could well have been bitten by hyaenas, by another lion, or even by a zebra she had caught. In line with the normal policy on injuries, the lioness was left to fend for herself. After a few months the tail was no better; it had become bent into an ugly rigid maggot-infested loop, painful for the lioness and distressing to the many tourists and others who saw her. Plainly she was likely neither to die of her injury nor to recover completely from it. In these circumstances I persuaded the park warden not to shoot her as he proposed; instead I immobilized her and the vet removed the tail, leaving a short but tidy stump. As a result, Masai female 14, now inevitably named Stumptail by the tourist guides, recovered fully. She is elderly now, at fifteen, and it shows. Her once sharp curved white teeth have turned into blunt toffee-coloured projections from her ageing gums. She has a drawn appearance about her face, and a gait which suggests that gravity is somewhat stronger for her than for younger lionesses. A festering ulcer on her tawny flank took a long time to heal, perhaps partly because she had no tail with which to whisk flies from it. She has outlived all the other lionesses who were in her pride when she was born in 1963, and she has seen her pride change ownership at least five times, as successive groups of males have taken and held possession of it for a while. They were mostly fine specimens, these temporary Serengeti sovereigns, lions with large flowing manes, dark and menacing or blonde and beautiful, lions whose roars rumbled through the starry nights, and whose grey flanks panted through the hot dusty days. They have all left their genetical mark and passed on.

For me, Masai female 14 symbolizes much of my knowledge of lions, some of which I have tried to convey in this book. She has lived long and contributed well to some of the best-documented case histories of wild mammals, revealing some of the complexities of the lions' fascinating social system. She has mated repeatedly, langorously, noisily, and sometimes successfully, with a variety of virile males, has given birth in synchrony with her relatives, and has helped them in trying to rear the short-limbed, sandy-furred, crawling cubs into sleek, lithe lionesses or solid, hairy-headed young males. She has lived the communal co-operative life of a lion pride member, experiencing all its ups and downs. The ups would be the sight of a black, seething wildebeest herd preparing to plunge through her patch of vegetation and emerge one

245

fewer, the warm smell of a newly killed zebra after several days of stomach-shrinking fasting, or the scampering and rustling sounds of well-fed cubs playing in a cool patch of shade. The downs would be the sharp pain of an *Acacia* thorn in a paw pad, the trailing behind yet another escaping supper, the theft of a small hard-won meal by a male, and the powerful and strange smell of intruding males challenging the present holders and offering a threat to the well-being of the future generation. Through all these changing fortunes, this lioness and her companions have managed at irregular intervals to capture and consume many equally beautiful wild animals of other species, and have made many more run for and with their lives. She has helped in alarming rival predators – the neighbouring prides as well as leopards, cheetahs and hyaenas. She and her pride have given pleasure to the countless thousands of tourists fortunate enough to have visited the Serengeti. I fervently hope that many thousands more, of different races and of distant generations, will be able to admire this most magnificent of the world's wildlife areas, carefully guarded by the Tanzanian National Parks organization. They will see Masai female 14's descendants, and although she herself will soon have died of old age, during her life she has contributed towards providing genes for future lions – and enjoyable and stimulating work for lionologists.

111 Three lionesses at dusk watch for potential prey

Further reading

BOOKS

DAWKINS, R. (1976), *The selfish gene*, Oxford University Press, Oxford.
A most readable book which describes in detail our present understanding of how natural selection operates – by favouring successful genes. Richard Dawkins takes much further some of the points I have touched on in Chapter 10.

EATON, R.L. (1972), *The cheetah: the biology, ecology and behavior of an endangered species*, Van Nostrand Reinhold Co., New York.
The title well summarizes the book, which in turn summarizes most aspects of what was known about cheetahs a few years ago. It lays much emphasis on Eaton's own observations of cheetahs in American safari parks.

GUGGISBERG, C.A.W. (1961), *Simba: the life of the lion*, Howard Timmins, Cape Town.
Before the days of full-time scientific field studies, Guggisberg described his observations of lions in Nairobi National Park. *Simba* (which is Swahili for 'lion') also outlines some of its author's encyclopaedic knowledge of the fascinating older literature on lions in history, culture and superstition.

GUGGISBERG, C.A.W. (1975), *Wild cats of the world*, David & Charles, Newton Abbot.
Now he has done the same, although naturally in less detail, for all the thirty-five species of wild cats in the world. A useful collection of what is known – and often very little is – and a reference book which is a pleasure to read.

KRUUK, H. (1972), *The spotted hyena: a study of predation and social behaviour,* Chicago University Press, Chicago.

The results of Hans Kruuk's years of study of hyaenas in the Serengeti and Ngorongoro; a wealth of data on the hunting methods and social organization of this maligned social carnivore.

KRUUK, H. (1975), *Hyaena,* Oxford University Press, Oxford.

The result of the same work presented in fine simple pictorial form, with many superb photographs illustrating the concise text on the hyaena, its predation and its environment.

MECH, L.D. (1970), *The wolf: the ecology and behavior of an endangered species,* Natural History Press, New York.

Another fine summary of knowledge about another much maligned social hunter, including many of the results of Mech's own work on wolves.

MOSS, C. (1976), *Portraits in the wild,* Hamish Hamilton, London.

Cynthia Moss has succeeded in bringing together into one readable book the results of recent field studies of the major species of East African mammals.

MOUNTFORT, G. (1973), *Tigers,* David & Charles, Newton Abbot.

Largely pictorial and in colour, this slim book is oriented towards the conservation of these magnificent threatened cats. It outlines the small amount which is known about their distribution, ecology and behaviour.

MYERS, N. (1975), *The cheetah Acinonyx jubatus in Africa;* MYERS, N. (1976), *The leopard Panthera pardus in Africa,* IUCN Monographs Nos 4 & 5, International Union for the Conservation of Nature and Natural Resources, Morges.

Norman Myers carried out an Africa-wide survey for IUCN of the present status and probable future of cheetahs and leopards. These reports are his results. They do not make encouraging reading (unless you hate cats), but they are useful and authoritative.

SCHALLER, G.B. (1972), *The Serengeti lion: a study of predator-prey relations,* Chicago University Press, Chicago.

The results of George Schaller's three-year study of lions in the Serengeti. His book gives a mass of useful data, particularly on predation, from his very many hours of observation of lions and other predators.

VAN LAWICK, H. & VAN LAWICK-GOODALL, J. (1971), *Innocent killers*, Houghton Mifflin, Boston.
> Close observation of families of hyaenas, jackals and wild dogs yielded some interesting descriptions of the different personalities and ways of life of the individual animals involved, as well as some truly magnificent photographs.

SCIENTIFIC PAPERS

BERTRAM, B.C.R. (1973), Lion population regulation, *East African Wildlife Journal*, Vol. 11, pp. 215–25.

BERTRAM, B.C.R. (1975), Social factors influencing reproduction in wild lions, *Journal of Zoology, London*, Vol. 177, pp. 463–82.

BERTRAM, B.C.R. (1976), Kin selection in lions and in evolution, in *Growing Points in Ethology* (edited by P.P.G. Bateson & R.A. Hinde), Cambridge University Press, pp. 281–301.

BERTRAM, B.C.R. & KING, J.M. (1976), Lion and leopard immobilization using CI-744, *East African Wildlife Journal*, Vol. 14, pp. 237–9.

ELOFF, F.C. (1973), Ecology and behavior of the Kalahari lion, in *The World's Cats*, Vol. 1 (edited by R.L. Eaton), World Wildlife Safari, Winston, Oregon, pp. 90–126.

JOSLIN, P. (1973), Factors associated with decline of the Asiatic lion, in *The World's Cats*, Vol. 1 (edited by R.L. Eaton), World Wildlife Safari, Winston, Oregon, pp. 127–41.

KRUUK, H. (1976), Feeding and social behaviour of the striped hyaena (*Hyaena vulgaris* Desmarest), *East African Wildlife Journal*, Vol. 14, pp. 91–111.

MUCKENHIRN, N.A. & EISENBERG, J.F. (1973), Home ranges and predation of the Ceylon leopard, in *The World's Cats*, Vol. 1 (edited by R.L. Eaton), World Wildlife Safari, Winston, Oregon, pp. 142–75.

RUDNAI, J. (1973), Reproductive biology of lions (*Panthera leo massaica* Neumann) in Nairobi National Park, *East African Wildlife Journal*, Vol. 11, pp. 241–53.

RUDNAI, J. (1974), The pattern of lion predation in Nairobi Park, *East African Wildlife Journal*, Vol. 12, pp. 213–25.

SCHALLER, G.B. (1968), Hunting behaviour of the cheetah in the Serengeti National Park, Tanzania, *East African Wildlife Journal*, Vol. 6, pp. 95–100.

SEIDENSTICKER, J.C., HORNOCKER, M.G., WILES, W.V. & MESSICK, J.P. (1973), Mountain lion social organization in the Idaho Primitive Area, *Wildlife Monographs*, No. 35, pp. 1–60.

SMUTS, G.L. (1976), Population characteristics and recent history of lions in two parts of the Kruger National Park, *Koedoe*, Vol. 19, pp. 153–64.

TAYLOR, C.R. & ROWNTREE, V.J. (1973), Temperature regulation and heat balance in running cheetahs: a strategy for sprinters?, *American Journal of Physiology*, Vol. 224, pp. 848–51.

Index

(Entries such as 'cubs', or 'ageing' refer to lions unless stated otherwise.)

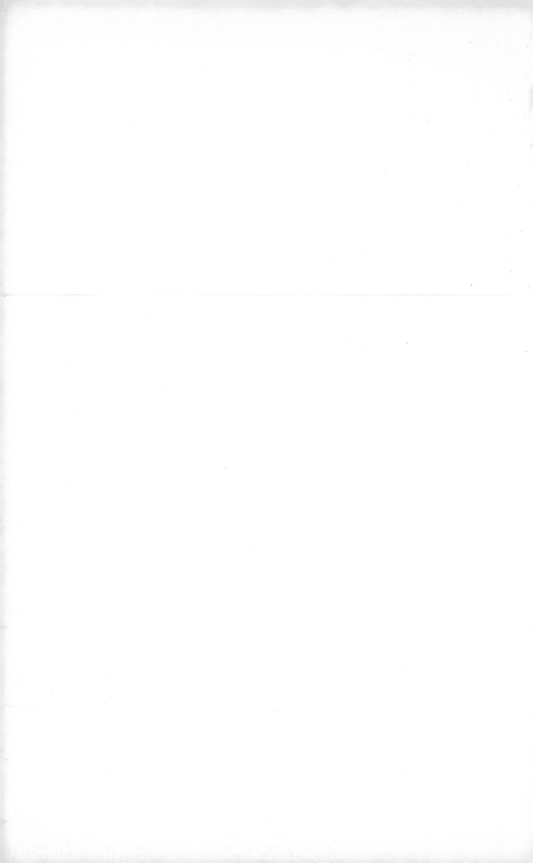